THE
DECORATIVE
ARTIST

THE DECORATIVE ARTIST

Yvonne Rees

HEADLINE

A QUARTO BOOK

First published in Great Britain in 1988 by
HEADLINE BOOK PUBLISHING PLC
Headline House
79 Great Titchfield Street
London W1P 7FN

British Library Cataloguing in Publication Data

Rees, Yvonne
    The decorative artist.
    1. Interior design
    I. Title
    747

ISBN 0-7472-0080-7

This book was designed and produced by
Quarto Publishing plc
The Old Brewery
6 Blundell Street
London N7 9BH

Senior Editor Denis Kennedy
Project Editor Diana Mansour

Designer Terry Smith
Design Stylist Ursula Dawson

Picture Researcher Joanna Wiese
Illustrators Graham Rosewarne, Craig Austin
Photographer Martin Hill

Art Director Moira Clinch
Editorial Director Carolyn King

Typeset by Ampersand Typesetting Limited, Bournemouth
Manufactured in Hong Kong by Regent Publishing Services Ltd
Printed in Hong Kong by South Sea Int'l Press Ltd.

CONTENTS

INTRODUCTION

The decorative arts have been with us since our prehistoric ancestors first daubed their walls with figures. Later, rugs, pots, furniture and even weapons from every culture across the world were decorated with patterns, pictures and colours. Whether the designs were applied for magical, religious or purely decorative reasons, there is no type of surface that hasn't at some time or in some part of the world been painted, carved, etched or embroidered. In fact, the material is immaterial. Traditional designs follow the shape and size of the object; they are boldly executed and fearlessly displayed. There is a form of folk art for everything and everyone: it is applied to everyday items and anyone can do it. Once learned, the techniques are not difficult and are more the province of the enthusiastic home-maker than of the painstaking professional.

Look at the history of folk art and you will find patterns and pictures recurring from century to century, and simultaneously in one civilization and another, even though their paths may not have crossed until recent times. There are florals, abstracts and stylized figures; some have a traditional significance, others are popular simply for their decorative value. All can be successfully adapted to your own home and its accessories by following our clear instructions. We show you how to prepare your surface and plan your pattern, create your own designs and work with today's easy-to-use paints.

If you have never thought of yourself as being artistically gifted, but have always fancied 'having a go', you will surprise yourself with our patterns and guidelines for easy to paint techniques. The correct movement of the hand or stroke of the brush will produce exactly the desired effect every time; simple rules on the use of colour will give a professional look to shaping and shading. In this book you will find instructions for decorating all kinds of surfaces, from walls and woodwork to fabric and china.

Be inspired – there are lots of projects and exciting ideas to copy – and, above all, have fun. If you follow the guidelines carefully, your home can only benefit!

Left *This dried and hollowed-out gourd obviously suggested the perfect shape for folk border painting using both floral and abstract designs in strong colours against a black background.*

Top right *Traditionally, every surface would be hand painted including walls, woodwork and furniture as this beautiful Norwegian interior demonstrates. Note the detailing over the door frames.*

Bottom left *You will find certain colour combinations used again and again like the blue/gold of this exquisite cabinet.*

Bottom right *The use of panels surrounded by decorative borders provided the opportunity to paint scenes, figures and animals.*

CHOOSING AND USING PATTERNS

The projects in this book offer a wealth of design ideas, from abstracts to flowers, fruit and figures. Some of these you may wish to use as they stand or they can be adapted to suit the objects in your home. You may, on the other hand, have several ideas for original projects of your own.

This section is designed to give practical advice about putting your own ideas into practice. The first step is to select the style of pattern that is most appropriate to your items: a painted fruit panel in the centre of your kitchen units, for example, or Delft-style figures on a bathroom tile. There are instructions for scaling a pattern up or down and for creating your own designs.

A successful pattern can be adjusted to fit a variety of objects, which may be either two or three dimensional. There are useful tips on altering patterns to fit the scale and shape of the object, and a guide to common design errors that can easily be avoided.

Colours should be chosen with equal care, given the bewilderingly wide range of modern paints and techniques. The guidelines given here will help you to use colour successfully in both traditional and modern projects.

Assimilate this information and you will understand how the projects given later in the book were designed and put together, and you will be able to tackle your own creations with confidence.

SELECTING A DECORATIVE STYLE

The pictures in this book and objects you may have already seen in shops, museums or magazines will give you some idea of the immense range of modern and traditional styles that can be employed on virtually anything from walls and floors to furniture, fabrics and ceramics. But why choose a particular pattern or colour for your own project; where and how should you use it, and on what kind of item?

Firstly, remember you are doing it for *fun*, so if you haven't tackled this kind of thing before, choose one of the patterns that is easy to execute, and experiment on something that doesn't matter, just in case your first attempts don't turn out quite as you'd hoped. Painting a giant cloth and matching napkins merely hours before your guests arrive, or putting your brush to a rather expensive item of second-hand furniture is not likely to create the sort of atmosphere that will relax the beginner and encourage good results. Give yourself the time and space to dabble, and try out some of the techniques first on a piece of card or old newspaper, or on a fabric offcut. If you fancy decorating furniture, pick up some cheap second-hand bargains for your first experiments and use these as test pieces.

Making patterns

Above all, allow yourself the time to read the book and instructions carefully, taking proper note of the chapters on preparation and on choosing the right materials. It is easy to be carried away by enthusiasm, but shortcuts lead to frustration and unsatisfactory results; although this type of free-hand painting is nothing like an exact science, there are tips and techniques that are essential if you are to achieve the correct effects. Once these have been learned, you can stretch your wings a little, try out your own ideas and make up your own patterns. Guidance for those who wish to create their own patterns, plus suggested projects for all levels of experience, are contained among the project and pattern pages.

It may be that you simply take a fancy to a particular pattern – an exotic abstract, a favourite cartoon figure or a floral perhaps – and are looking for something on which to paint. Alternatively, you may have quite specific design plans for an article in the home which you would like to decorate by hand; in this case your choice of colour and design will be limited to those in your general scheme and you will be looking out for the right pattern. The designs and projects in this book are arranged according to their motif: figures, birds and animals, flowers, fruit and abstract designs. You will see from the photographs why certain objects presented themselves as ideal for a particular pattern: pretty flowers on an old-fashioned country-style chest of drawers, for example; animals and figures for a child's room, or fruit for the kitchen.

Folk art

In the early days of hand painting for the home it was often just the shape of an object that suggested its painted design, and this approach may well trigger off a creative decision. Thus ivy may creep up the legs of a chair or a vine describe a frieze around your dining room walls. Scenic pictures are ideal for a wide, flat surface like a tray, box or chest; fruit and flowers for the focal point of an object like the back of a chair, a cupboard panel or the centre of a plate. Geometric designs or trailing foliage lend themselves perfectly to rims, edges and spouts. Sometimes, the choice of pattern or picture may be dictated by tradition: for example, Russian religious ikons, Norway's floral *Rosemaling* decoration or the canal boatmen's Van Dyking. In this last case, household objects and boat panels were decorated with stylized roses and daisies arranged around a panel depicting dogs, churches and, usually, castles. A Van-Dyked panel would generally have certain ingredients: a hilly landscape behind, a sea or lake in the distance, and water in the foreground, complete with boats, trees, a bridge and some swans. Romany paintwork tends to be more baroque, with plenty of scrolls and symbolic leaves, and horses' heads are usually an element of the design. If you wish to pursue an authentic historical theme – on your own canal boat, perhaps, or on antique furniture – you will have to research your subject matter thoroughly in specialist books and in museums before you can turn your findings into practical designs.

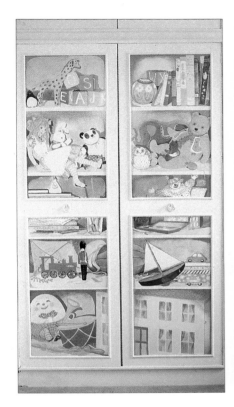

If you want to reproduce a traditional piece like the bargee's tinware, a wedding coffer or military chest, your chosen colours and designs must be dictated by historical limitations and you will need to research your piece carefully in specialist books and museums before you start. Sometimes, an antique piece will be the inspiration for a completely different design like the plate which inspired the pattern for the small tin with lid, **above***. Other ideas could be sparked off by anything you see or use everyday,*

or be suggested by the very shape of the object you wish to decorate. Thus leaves and flowers may entwine themselves up and across a bureau; a botanical or zoological reference book provide pictures to copy onto fabric or ceramic; or a child's comic or story book illustration be transferred onto nursery furniture. The painted objects **above** *will give you some idea of the wide range of items and designs that could be employed. But you will no doubt have lots of ideas of your own.*

SCALE AND POSITION

If your chosen design or pattern is to look right, it must be in proportion to your object and suited to its shape. If the design is too big, it will swamp the object on which it is painted and both will look ridiculous; if a pattern or motif is too small, then it will be insignificant and difficult to see. One of the most common mistakes is to paint a too-modest frieze around a room with a high ceiling, where any design must be of generous proportions if it is to be noticed. Another error, and one which it is all too easy to make, is to fail to plan carefully, so that instead of having an even number of repeats along a wall, there is an awkward half-repeat at one corner. Trial and error is an infuriating and time-consuming way of learning, and it can be avoided if you plan ahead and calculate exactly what adjustments are required: instructions for scaling a pattern up or down are given later.

Assessing the scale
To gauge the ideal size for a motif, the best thing is to see it in place: sketch it on tracing paper and then scale it up and down until you have several samples of varying sizes. These can be used not only to choose the correct scale but also for positioning. Tape a sample in place, if necessary, so that you can stand back and see the effect from a distance; or you may find it easier to use the roughs as templates and mark the various samples temporarily, using chalk. This will enable you to explore the different ways in which a pattern can be used.

To plan a design in relation to the object on which it is to be placed, look at the latter carefully and decide whether it has a centre or a clear focal point; for example, the seat or back of a chair, the centre of a tablemat, a panel or a chimney breast. If there is no obvious focal point, perhaps a repeat pattern would be more appropriate – along a dado rail, circling a tubular object such as a tin or jar, and so on. Some items will obviously lend themselves to both effects.

With a centred design, positioning is simply a matter of making the design fit the allotted space neatly, bearing in mind that the effect may need to be repeated over a series of panels or on several plates or tiles. You won't have to worry about getting the painted effect exactly identical each time – slight variations are part of the charm of free-hand painting – but you should take the trouble to centre your pattern exactly. Use chalk to measure and mark the exact centre point, making sure that the pattern is symmetrically placed.

Accurate positioning and preplanning is even more essential in the case of repetitive or circular designs, where it is necessary to work out in advance how many full repeats can be fitted into the space. Measure the length of the strip that is to be decorated and then draw it to scale on squared paper. Find the central point and work out how many repeats will fall on either side; you may find that it is necessary to adjust the pattern in order to have complete pattern repeats. If the pattern is to run around the walls of a room or a three-dimensional object that is square or rectangular – a box or chest, for example – one way of adjusting a pattern to fit is to design a separate, but complementary, corner pattern, enabling you to turn the corners neatly.

Circular designs
For a circular design the pattern must be calculated exactly so that each section is complete and the pattern is continuous. This is easily done by dividing the object into segments and positioning a pattern portion into each segment. With a large pattern or too many segments, you may find that the pattern does not run comfortably round the curve, in which case your design will have to be adjusted. If you find you can't use the standard plastic protractor because the degrees are too closely marked for accuracy, make your own measuring and marking device using a circle of stiff board or plywood divided into 10 degree sections. This can be laid on your item and the required divisions marked off.

Make your positioning marks with chalk which can easily be rubbed off after painting. Only use pencil for a design with fine detail – pencil marks can be difficult to remove and the point sometimes indents soft woods.

Above *Small, simple motifs, like the hearts and flowers used above, can be arranged and rearranged to fit objects of many different sizes, so that you can continue a theme around a room.*

Below *It is always worth taking time to check that the scale is right and that the different elements in an arrangement are well organized. Working from left to right and top to bottom, the design works reasonably well on the first drawer; on the next it is too large; then, the elements are*

spaced too far apart; the next design is too small; the leaves and corn stalks at the bottom left drawer are too straight, and finally, the flowers are all facing inwards and the stalks are curving up instead of down as in a natural flower arrangement.

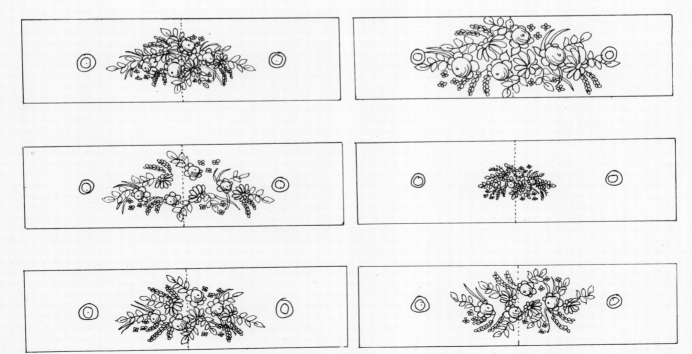

13

CREATING YOUR OWN PATTERNS

If you don't want to use any of the designs supplied in this book, or have some creative ideas of your own, you don't need any special drawing skills to produce your own patterns. Keep your design relatively simple, translating it into a basic outline or shape – further details can be added with free-hand painting or with secondary templates at a later stage – and virtually any pattern can be adapted for your own use. To transfer the pattern to paper or card, simply trace over the outlines or cut out the shape, simplifying it as required before scaling it up or down to the correct size, as already described.

In some cases a slide projector can be a valuable tool. Simply project the outline of the pattern or motif onto a piece of paper taped to the wall so that you can draw the outline to scale and at the same time adapt it to a workable pattern, using the lens adjustment to enlarge or reduce it to the desired size. This is a particularly useful technqiue for transferring a design for a mural onto the wall.

Sources

Everything around you, from pictures in books and magazines to everyday objects, may be used to suggest possible designs. The following will give you some starting points:

● Pattern books – both old and new pattern books are readily available and designs can be traced for a wide range of modern and traditional styles. Both wallpaper and specialist stencil pattern books can be adapted to make templates for free-hand painting.
● You can draw round an actual object such as a leaf, fruits sliced lengthwise to give a flat surface, or cups, saucers and plates, to make circular shapes. Keep your eyes open for everyday objects with interesting shapes and experiment with them to see how they can be arranged to create patterns.
● Raid the children's toybox for building blocks, unusual shapes and other simple learning toys that might make excellent templates.
● Pastry cutters come in all shapes and sizes perfect for ready-made templates.
● Greetings cards are a good source of simple designs which can be cut out easily and used.

● Use the stylized geometrics of oriental rugs and carpets as the basis of an abstract design or check out other historical patterns as far back as the Greek key border or Etruscan motifs. South American, Indian and Persian folk arts are good sources of stylized figures, birds and animals which can be found on simply woven fabrics, pictures and handicrafts.

You can use all of these sources to find shapes and designs which can be juggled and reassembled to create patterns. For a neat outline, don't forget to use the appropriate drawing aids: a pair of compasses, a ruler (metal if you are cutting along the edge with a knife), a flexible rule (for drawing curves) and a set square for sharp angles. While the painting technique may not be exact, the end result will have a more professional look if the basic design is accurately drawn. A tip for symmetrical shapes like circles, ovals or butterflies is to fold a sheet of paper then draw one half of the design only, using the fold as the centre line of the full design, then cut out the design through both layers of paper. When it is opened out, the two sides will be accurate mirror images.

Above *Some 'found' patterns seem ready-made for drawing around, like this ornamental, metal iron stand.*

Right *Keep your eye open for interesting shapes – even pastry cutters – and colour combinations from tiles, papers, fabrics or books.*

SIZING AND APPLYING A PATTERN

In this book, you will find lots of suggestions for patterns, some of which you may like to try out for yourself. Later, we shall be looking at how you can make your own patterns and try out original creative ideas. Firstly though, you must learn how to scale a pattern up or down for, as we have seen, correct scale and size are essential to success, and patterns are rarely exactly right. Don't be tempted to make do through a natural impatience to put your ideas into action; if you fall into this trap you will inevitably be disappointed by the results.

There are several ways in which a pattern can be made larger or smaller. The quickest and easiest method is to take the pattern to the nearest photocopying service that has a machine sophisticated enough to do enlargements and reductions. You will need to know exactly how large or how small the pattern must be, in order to avoid expensive trial-and-error return visits. Alternatively, you can more laboriously do the job yourself using a pantograph – an adjustable device that looks like a series of hinged rulers and that will make enlarged or reduced copies from any original. To use a pantograph, you simply trace over the original with the point at one end, and the lead at the other end of the pantograph will simultaneously make a copy to the required size.

Scaling to a grid
If you don't have access to a photocopying machine or a pantograph, you will have to use the 'longhand' method of rescaling your design. This involves drawing a simple grid of squares over the original and plotting each section of pattern into the appropriate square of a grid that has been scaled up or down. Even if you have no previous drawing skills, copying the small section of a picture that falls within the confines of a square is infinitely easier than attempting to copy the whole, and you will be surprised at the success of the results.

When you have planned and rescaled your pattern, you can plot it onto your object. Your pattern can be applied in one of two ways depending on how intricate it is. You can draw it on a piece of card or paper and cut out the complete design, rather like a stencil, before mapping it onto your object. Alternatively, cut out simpler, individual shapes to make templates, as you would for cutting patchwork. Breaking down a design into its component parts and making templates of it sometimes helps to create a more flexible and fluid design, as the templates can be re-arranged in different combinations and positions. Where a pattern is to be repeated many times, or where the design is intricate and you wish to save it for possible future use, your pattern should be drawn on a durable surface such as stout card (afterwards varnished) or stiff brown manilla paper brushed with linseed oil and left to dry to create a tough, waterproof material.

Remember, too, that masking tape is useful for isolating panels ready for painting, and for making straight guidelines when drawing simple patterns. The masking tape can be pulled away when the decoration is finished, leaving a clear-cut edge.

Marking the design
As for marking centre points and other guidelines, chalk is the best and most easily removable marker for most surfaces, though it is not always suitable for fine detail. For timber, you can use an old biro from which the ink has run out, though you will have to take care not to indent the surface too deeply. In the case of certain fabrics, you can transfer the design by making a series of pinpricks on a paper pattern, using a needle set into a cork and following the lines of the design; once you have gone over the design, lay the paper pattern on the fabric and brush powdered chalk over it, marking the fabric beneath. For ceramics and glass, use a chinagraph pencil, which is easily rubbed off after painting – take care to draw slightly outside your desired line when using one of these as you will not be able to paint over the chinagraph line.

It is surprisingly easy to scale a pattern up or down. The simplest method is to use a photocopier with this facility. If this is not possible, a pantograph is a very effective instrument: all that is needed is to set the pins at the correct scale then run the outliner around the lines of the original. The marker will simultaneously draw the same lines to the larger scale. Equally effective is a grid, drawn to a larger or smaller scale than the grid placed over the original. For a complicated design, make a dot where each design line crosses a grid line, then simply join the dots to reproduce the original.

COLOUR SELECTION

When the choice of colour for home decoration was limited to local pigments, it was easy to select a scheme – painters generally chose the brightest colours and put them against a dark background. This made the bright colours almost luminous, and so lightened their often gloomy rooms. These days, there is a wide range of colours and the opportunity to use reliable, specially formulated paints with the result that the choice is almost infinite and it can be difficult to know where to start. Oil and water-based paints can be bought in handy tubes or tubs and mixed to produce the shade you need, and even ready mixed household paint comes in a choice of up to 400 or more options. To ensure that you buy only the colours you need and that those you use look good together, it makes sense to plan your scheme carefully.

Colours in folk art
First, decide on the general effect you are hoping to achieve: if you are planning a traditional hand-painted piece it is important to choose the right colours for an authentic feel. You will find our forebears used a very limited palette: folk artists in North and West Rumania, for example, used only red, black and brown, rarely blue, while those in southern Rumania favoured red and green combinations. A characteristic of the Lower Rhine area was white or yellow pattern on a red or reddish brown background. American tole painting is enjoying a revival of interest: a form of brush stroke painting prevalent in New England and among the Pennsylvanian Dutch (hence the strong German influence), tole painting favours bright colours, mainly vermilion, yellow, green and black, often highlighted with gold or silver leaf. Gilt stencilling was a popular early American shortcut, designed to imitate the gilded carvings and brasswork found on furniture from Europe's Empire period.

Van Dyking
The Victorian canalboat dwellers employed the same principles for their Van Dyking: handpainting every available surface with light colours on a dark background as an inexpensive form of decoration.

Even the boats themselves had an inflexible colour scheme: a dark colour (usually red) along the centre, with blue or green above and the roof painted with plain red oxide. To this would be added the familiar multicoloured pictures and lettering – bright but never gaudy against the dark background. Inside, indifferent timber panelling would be given an undercoat of buff yellow and was then combgrained with light oak scumble for a more sophisticated and even finish. The mouldings were picked out in red and the cupboard doors in green.

Of course, with large modern windows and efficient electric lighting, our homes no longer need the vivid contribution of such bright colours, and unless you particularly want to reproduce an old-fashioned piece or design, there's no reason why you should not translate your patterns into pastel shades or colours specially chosen to coordinate with other interior decorations.

If you find it difficult to blend colours, adopt a professional approach and use a colour wheel. Viewed simply, this divides into two halves: cool colours (blues and greens) and warm colours (reds and oranges). Start with the predominant colour in your room scheme: the colours on either side of it are those that harmonize best with it; the colours directly opposite are complementary and are the best to use for contrast. It is the colours in between that you should avoid – or at least use with discretion – as these will tend to clash. The colour wheel will help you plan a scheme that co-ordinates perfectly with your other decorations and furnishings.

The second consideration to bear in mind when harmonizing your design into a general scheme is the importance of getting exactly the right shade. Take extra care with choosing and blending colours, remembering that they look very different according to light, position and surface: the same blue on a shiny substance like a ceramic tile is going to look rather different on a soft one like fabric. Test your colours on offcuts and scraps, allowing your samples to dry completely before you use them to make colour decisions. This is particularly important when mixing acrylic colours, as these can change character quite dramatically when seen against a background colour.

When painting furniture, the colours may be dictated by the decorative scheme of your room. The pretty hand-painted chests, **left and below**, have picked up the blues, pinks and creams of the bedrooms where they are to be positioned. The bathroom wallpaper suggested the theme for the unit, **below right**. Fake antiques, **below left**, usually require traditional strong colour combinations.

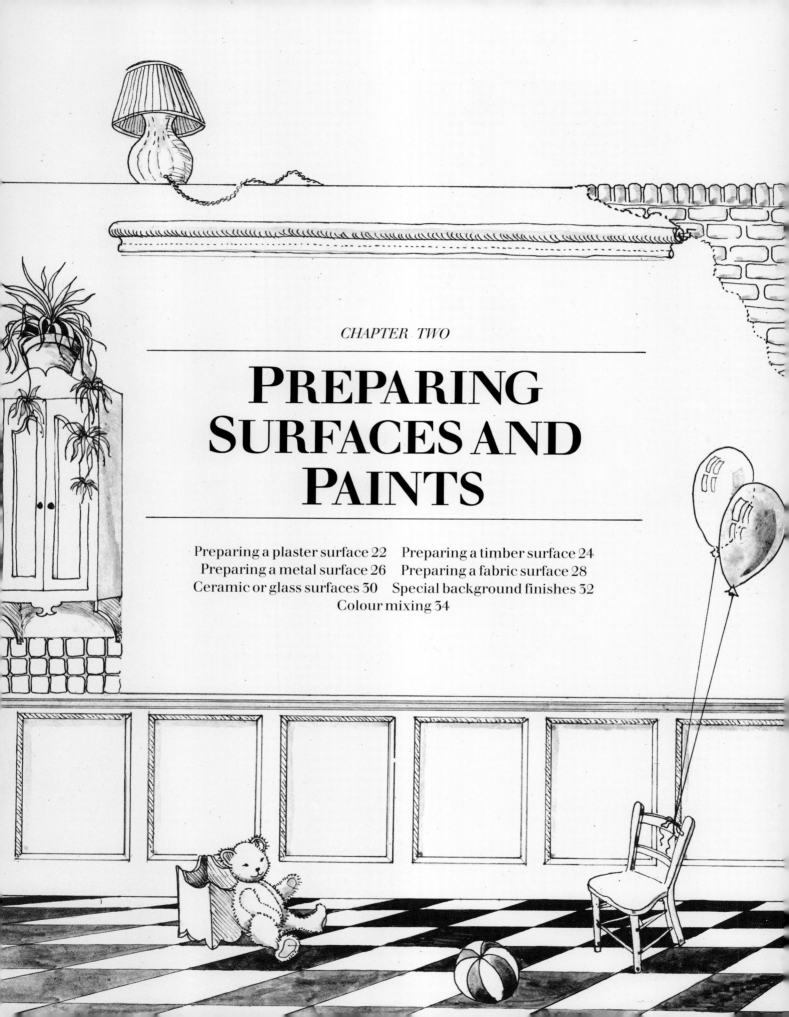

CHAPTER·TWO

PREPARING SURFACES AND PAINTS

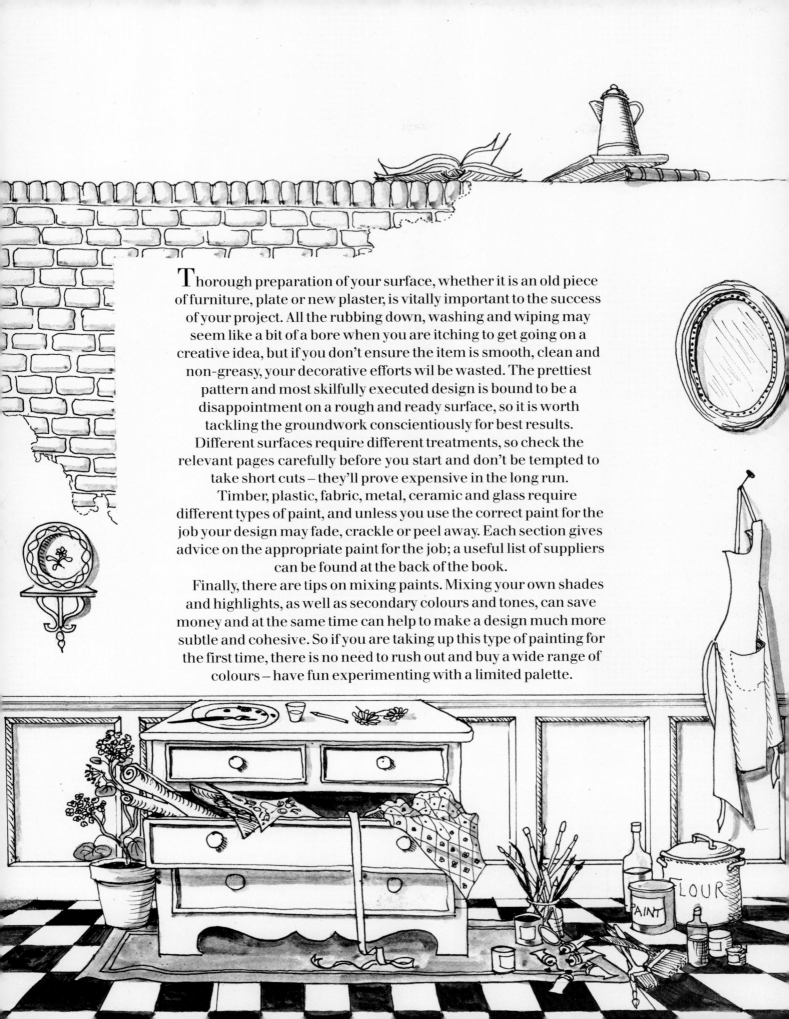

Thorough preparation of your surface, whether it is an old piece of furniture, plate or new plaster, is vitally important to the success of your project. All the rubbing down, washing and wiping may seem like a bit of a bore when you are itching to get going on a creative idea, but if you don't ensure the item is smooth, clean and non-greasy, your decorative efforts wil be wasted. The prettiest pattern and most skilfully executed design is bound to be a disappointment on a rough and ready surface, so it is worth tackling the groundwork conscientiously for best results.

Different surfaces require different treatments, so check the relevant pages carefully before you start and don't be tempted to take short cuts – they'll prove expensive in the long run.

Timber, plastic, fabric, metal, ceramic and glass require different types of paint, and unless you use the correct paint for the job your design may fade, crackle or peel away. Each section gives advice on the appropriate paint for the job; a useful list of suppliers can be found at the back of the book.

Finally, there are tips on mixing paints. Mixing your own shades and highlights, as well as secondary colours and tones, can save money and at the same time can help to make a design much more subtle and cohesive. So if you are taking up this type of painting for the first time, there is no need to rush out and buy a wide range of colours – have fun experimenting with a limited palette.

PREPARING A PLASTER SURFACE

A painted decoration on the wall is an excellent and inexpensive alternative to wallpaper, especially in older properties where the walls are often very irregular in shape, or a hand finish might be more appropriate to the style of the house. Before you start painting, it is absolutely essential to make sure that the surface is sound, or your creative efforts will be wasted. Repair any cracks, and check the condition of your walls for signs of damp – this must be traced back to source and rectified before you go any further. Damp may be caused externally by a leaking pipe or gutter, or it may creep up from the ground, in which case it is called rising damp. External leaks and rising damp should not be confused with condensation; this last is due to lack of ventilation in the home, causing moisture-laden air to condense on the nearest cold surface – your wall. Anti-condensation paint is available: use it under your painted finish to reduce condensation problems.

When you are confident that there is no risk of damp, you can start preparing a suitable wall surface; remember that it will have to be as clean and smooth as possible if you are painting it, as the slightest hairline crack will show through and spoil your decoration. Where an otherwise sound wall is covered in hairline cracks, the best option is probably to cover the wall in lining paper and paint over this. The alternative is an allover skim – or thin topcoat – of plaster. Occasional chips and small cracks can be filled and smoothed over. This is done by widening the crack slightly with the side of your filling knife and scraping out any loose particles. You must moisten the crack with water using a small paintbrush, then pack a proprietary filler into the crevice, making sure that it is well filled and leaving the filling slightly proud of the wall surface. When it has hardened, after a couple of hours, you can sand it to a smooth finish.

Where the wall is sound but has been previously painted, you should wash it down with sugar soap, diluted detergent or other proprietary paint cleaner to remove dirt, dust and grease. Wash from the top downwards to avoid runs and rinse well. Old whitewash or distemper is a different matter as it is too unstable and flaky to take paint well. Remove it by scrubbing. If the wall has been previously painted with gloss paint, key the surface by rubbing it with sandpaper or liquid sander, or, if it has started to peel, strip it off.

New plaster has to be left to dry out thoroughly and this usually takes several weeks; your builder should be able to advise you. Before painting, seal the surface with a recommended primer or with a thin coat of emulsion. New plasterboard requires a coat of plasterboard primer sealer. Old plasterboard can be repaired by patching any holes with a piece cut to fit and fixed in place with plaster or nails. Finish the area with a skim coat of plaster to hide the joins.

Suitable paints

Emulsion, a vinyl-based paint, is ideal for using on plaster – it dries quickly and is soluble in water yet provides a tough, wipe-down finish. Emulsion is available in a matt or sheen finish and comes in liquid, jellied or solid form. Its quick-drying properties are particularly useful when you are applying a difficult pattern involving the use of several colours.

Eggshell paint is also popular for use on walls. It covers well, helping to hide surface faults, and is solvent-based like gloss paint but with a soft sheen rather than high gloss finish. Gloss paint is more often used on metal and timber, but it can be used on walls to provide a rather hard, high gloss finish. Over large areas it tends to show up imperfections such as pitting or hollows.

Glazes can be used to dilute pigment colours for applying some of the special paint effects on pages 32-3. They produce a softer, more sheeny effect than diluted household paints.

Artists' colours, both oils and acrylics, can be applied to small areas of decoration, such as a frieze or for fine details. They would be expensive to use over large areas, but because they are available in small tubes or tubs, they are useful where only a small amount of a particular colour is required.

A painted wall can be just as decorative as wallpaper and a large, repeated motif quick and easy to accomplish.

For the more proficient painter, a trompe l'oeil effect can add an exciting new dimension to a dull room.

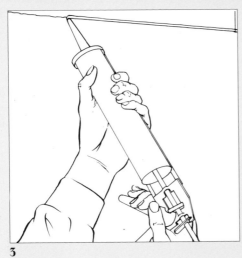

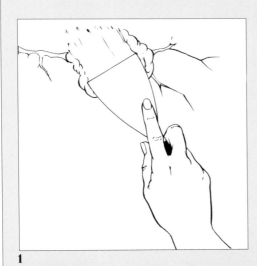

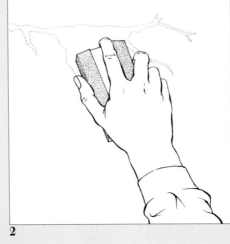

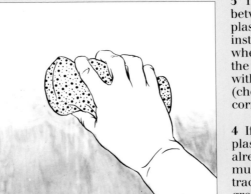

1 Large cracks must first be widened with the corner of a filling knife to remove loose or crumbly plaster. Use clear water and a brush to dampen the sides of the crack, then fill it with an all-purpose filler.

2 When the filler has started to harden, wipe over the top with a damp cloth, leaving the wall surface smooth and flat. When the filler has hardened completely, sand over the surface.

3 Troublesome cracks – between sheets of plasterboard, for instance, or at the angle where the ceiling meets the walls – can be filled with a flexible mastic (check that you have the correct formulation).

4 If you are decorating plasterwork that has already been painted you must first clean away all traces of grime and grease, using a cleaning agent such as sugar soap. Work from the top downwards to avoid runs.

PREPARING A TIMBER SURFACE

Furniture is perfectly suited to freehand decoration and a hand-painted cupboard, chest or chair will make a delightful addition to your home. The very shape of your piece will suggest all kinds of possibilities and you can tackle whatever suits your time, resources and capabilities, from a small trinket box to a huge cupboard or chest of drawers. You may wish to paint a piece of furniture or panelling that is already in your home; alternatively, it is fun to scour the junkyards for inexpensive bargains that can be transformed with a little paint.

If the wood has been previously painted and is in good condition, you can often paint straight over it, having first given the piece a good wash down and rinse with sugar soap or similar cleaner to remove any dirt and grease. Gloss paint should be gently rubbed or wiped with liquid sander to key the surface, and the same applies to a plain varnished surface.

Furniture can be stripped in one of several ways: you can send it away to be dipped in a tank of caustic soda for a fee. Be careful with old pieces as the soda sometimes weakens the glue and they may fall apart on their return. Always remove any handles or decorative trims before dipping. Alternatively, you can do the job yourself at home with a proprietary paste or gelled chemical (wear rubber gloves) or by using a hot air gun. Whichever method you use, make sure that you stand the piece on plenty of layers of newspaper and that it is well washed and dried after stripping. A variety of strippers of different shapes are available to help with awkward shapes.

If you are giving your timber a bare, varnished surface, fill in any holes with wood filler or paste. Work this well into the surface with a filling knife and allow it to set before sanding it down and staining it to match the wood. To ensure a smooth surface, both new and old wood should be sanded down, washed, and sanded again, using the finest grade of sandpaper. Brush any knots in the wood with shellac to prevent the resin leaching through your painted finish. If you are going for a natural finish, stain and varnish the wood, taking the time to apply the varnish thinly in several coats. Allow each coat to dry thoroughly and sand it down before applying the next.

An all-over painted finish will require a coating of primer (oil or water based) or tole sealer (a transparent varnish suitable for either a plain or painted finish), to prevent the paint sinking into the porous timber. Particularly resinous woods may require a special aluminium primer. Gloss paint also requires an undercoat – choose the colour recommended for your particular topcoat and apply evenly. It is sometimes necesssary to apply more than one undercoat in order to get good coverage and provide a smooth finish for the gloss.

Suitable paints
Gloss paint is ideal for timber, providing a high gloss finish. It is good for a base coat but too messy to use on complicated patterns. The non-drip gel type avoids runs. Gloss paint is also slow to dry.

Eggshell paint is similar to gloss but produces a softer sheeny finish.

Special paints like the silk vinyl ranges and new wood paints produce an attractive soft satin finish and do not require an undercoat. You may find that these are limited to the more fashionable pastel colours.

Enamels and japan paints produce a very hard, high-gloss finish that has to be applied with care, and the japan paints are generally best used for a base coat rather than for detail. Neither type blends well and they produce a hard, clearly defined edge. Similar, cellulose-based paints, like those used on cars, are available in spray cans.

Artists' colours, both oil and acrylic, can be used where only small amounts of colour are required, providing the timber has been primed.

Above *A fine example of Norwegian flower painting or* Rosemaling *on an antique wooden chest.*

Left *More contemporary florals have been used to brighten up stripped floors and timber units in the kitchen.*

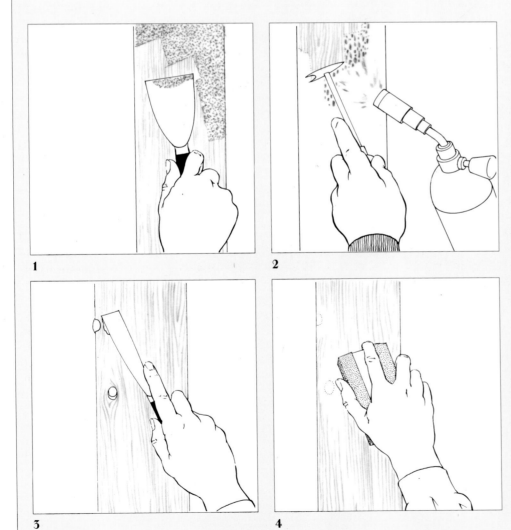

1 To use a chemical stripper, first make sure that the room is well aired and clear from pets or children. Paint the liquid liberally over the surface, using a paintbrush. When the paint begins to blister, remove it with a paint stripper, putting the scrapings in a metal container.

2 To use a blowtorch, play the flame lightly over the surface until the paint starts to bubble, then scrape it away with a shavehook or scraper. Wear thick gloves and sweep up regularly.

3 Holes or cracks in a timber surface must be filled with wood stopper. Use a flexible filling knife to force the stopper into the hole. On a corner, fill from one side and then the other.

4 Fill to just above the surface then, when the stopper has dried, sand it flush to the surface, using fine sandpaper wrapped around a sanding block.

Preparing a Metal Surface

Old iron objects, like ranges, flat irons and washboards, and tinware and enamelware, like mugs, jars and trays, are perfect for bright hand painting, set against a dark background in the style of early American tole painting or the Van Dyking employed by bargees. Rust is the scourge of metal objects and here more than with any other surface, great care must be taken to make conscientious preparations.

With an old metal object, never try to paint over signs of rust or it will reoccur and will break through the surface paint almost immediately. You must remove every trace with an emery cloth, steel wool pad or, over a large area, a wire cup brush or scouring wheel attached to an electric drill. A fibreglass repair kit can be used to repair holes after every trace of rust has been removed; rusted and pitted tinware can be prepared using naval jelly, following the instructions on the container. When the object has been completely cleaned of rust, dirt and grease, wash it in warm soapy water and allow it to dry thoroughly. Non-ferrous metal, such as aluminium or copper, should be washed with white spirit before priming.

New tin items must be cleaned with a half-and-half mixture of white vinegar and water to remove the oily coating that is applied for protection. Wash the items in warm soapy water, as for old metal, and dry them thoroughly. Both old and new objects can now be primed with an appropriate primer like red oxide, zinc chromate or, in the case of tin, a couple of coats of shellac applied 24 hours apart and sanded with fine sandpaper between coats. When your object has received a coat of rust preventative sealer, apply at least two coats of oil-based paint, either sprayed or brushed on in the colour of your choice – dark colours usually look the most effective. Do not be tempted to use a water-based paint as this tends to chip off easily with use. If you are using a flat enamel for your base coat, spray on a few coats of satin varnish to help your brush strokes to go on more easily over the top.

Suitable paints

Enamels like those used for model-making come in small tubs and a wide range of colours. They don't blend easily and tend to go on rather thickly, which makes them difficult to control if you are trying out special effects. They are expensive to use over large areas.

Cellulose-based paints come in pen, spray and can form and are mainly intended for repainting cars and boats. The colour range may be limited and they don't mix well, but sprays are useful for covering large areas evenly.

Ceramic paints can be used successfully on metal and come in a range of artists' colours which can be easily blended.

Enamel paints cover quickly in one coat and are ideal for large items like this bread bin.

Using a fine brush, they are equally good for producing a hand enamelled effect on smaller objects.

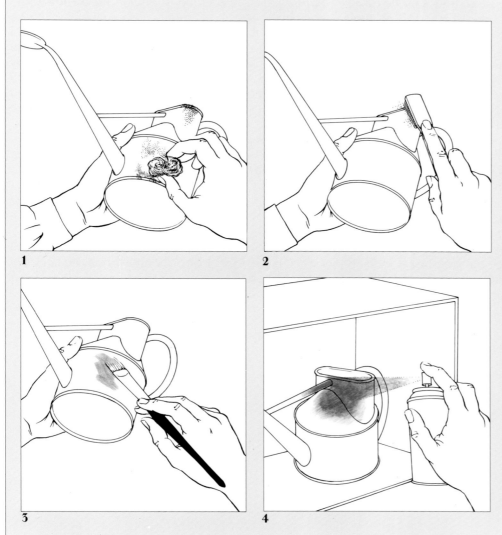

1 To prepare metalwork for painting, it should first be washed thoroughly and then rubbed down. This can be done with a steel wool pad or with a fine-grade silicone carbide paper.

2 If the surface is very rusted, all traces of rust must first be removed. Use a wire brush or – if you have one – a cup or wheel pattern wire brush fitted to an electric drill.

3 On a surface which is lightly rusted you can use a liquid rust remover. This is brushed onto the surface and left to dry. When it has fully dried, the rust should have been converted into a sound surface that can be primed and painted.

4 If an object is small, you can protect the surrounding area while you spray by removing the top flaps from a cardboard box, turning it on its side, and then standing the object within the box.

PREPARING A FABRIC SURFACE

Fabric paints offer the scope to experiment with your own designs on home furnishings, accessories and even your own clothes. Use them to create cushion panels, as insertions within co-ordinating fabric borders, to decorate plain lampshades or inexpensive fabric roller blinds, or to create original tablecloths with matching napkins and table mats. The more adventurous might like to create an edging or panel design that would be suitable for other soft furnishings, such as curtains or sofa covers. Children will love to find their favourite cartoon character transferred to the bib of their pinafore or dungarees, or you might design your own personalized T-shirt.

Wash and dry fabrics wherever possible to remove the manufacturer's dressing and test for shrinkage; items such as shades and blinds should be well brushed to remove dust and lint. It you wish to change the base colour of your fabric, it will have to be dyed with one of the proprietary fabric dyes that are available in a wide range of colours. Follow the manufacturer's instructions – some can be used easily in an automatic washing machine. Remember that some paints are designed to sink into the fibre of the fabric and if the background colour is dark this will darken the decorative painting. Other paints stay proud of the surface.

To provide a firm surface for painting, it helps to stretch the fabric taut over an embroidery frame. If you do not have a frame, tape the fabric to a table or worktop to create a taut surface.

Suitable paints

Fabric dyes are available in a wide range of permanent colours, usually applied by washing. Varied effects can be achieved by applying wax patterns (batik) or by scrumpling and tying the fabric so that parts escape the dye to create patterns (tie-dying).

Fabric paints also come in a wide range of colours and can be mixed to create your own shades. These are simply painted on and can be diluted, bearing in mind that this creates a much thinner, opaque look. Most can be heat-set after painting, usually by ironing, so that the fabric can be washed or dry cleaned without fear of the colours running. Some fabric paints are opaque but others are transparent.

Fabric pens offer fabric paint in a felt tip pen format in a limited range of colours and are useful for applying paint in finer detail.

Silk and wool paints are specially formulated for painting or printing on these fabrics. They are generally set by using a special fixative.

Glitter paints are useful for special effects and are available in a limited choice of colours. The fabric can be washed after the design has been set by ironing.

For would-be fashion designers, fabric paints provide an exciting way to design and decorate your own clothes. Why not experiment on plain white teeshirts and gym shoes, which cost you very little to buy and, being cotton, take the paint well?

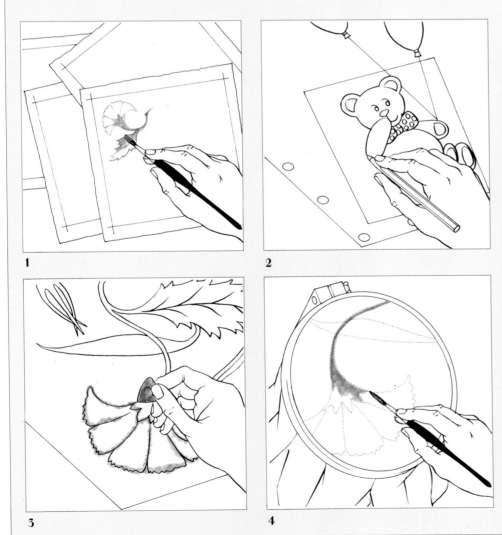

1 If you intend to paint several sections of fabric, mark out the pieces on the fabric, then transfer the design and paint it. Take care not to run into the seam allowances, marking these in with tailor's chalk.

2 One way of transferring a design is to use dressmaker's carbon paper. With large designs, make tracings of the different elements of the design and transfer the design in sections.

3 Chalk can also be used to mark a design. Make a tracing of the design then, on the reverse side, trace over the lines with a piece of tailor's chalk. Pin the tracing, chalked side down, over the fabric, then run over the lines with an empty ballpoint pen.

4 The fabric should be held taut during painting. Either pin or tape it to a board (put plenty of old newspaper underneath to absorb excess paint) or work with it in a hoop.

CERAMIC OR GLASS SURFACES

Ceramic and glass paints provide the opportunity to decorate plates, tiles, cups, glasses and vases with your own designs or to match other furnishings in the home. You may wish to coordinate cups or glasses to your cloth and tablemats, or perhaps transform a plain plate into an ornament to hang on the wall or stand in a rack. Painted ceramic items can be gently 'proved' in a warm oven so that they can be washed without fear of the design chipping off; however, they cannot be expected to be as tough and resilient as objects that have been fired after painting so hand-decorated items need to be handled with reasonable care.

Hand-painted designs are not very hard-wearing and would not be suitable for plates receiving a daily battering from knives and forks, for example, and such items should not be put into a dishwasher. Transparent glass paints can be used on ceramics or on glass, where they create stained-glass effects, particularly when combined with false lead strips, which are available by the roll. They can also be mixed with oil-based, opaque ceramic paints.

Items to be painted should be clean and free from grease. Wash them in warm soapy water or clean them with white spirit and rinse before painting. Brushes should also be washed in white spirit and completely dried before you start work with oil-based paints, or the water in the brush will produce unwelcome bubbles.

Suitable paints

Ceramic paints may be oil or water based and are used on china or glass for an opaque decorative effect. Oil-based paints are cold setting; water-based ones tend to require baking in the oven at low temperature for around 30 minutes. Both come in a good range of colours that can be mixed with other paints of the same type to make your own shades.

Glass paints can also be solvent or water based and come in a choice of colours that can be blended. Solvent-based glass paints can also successfully be used on aluminium and wood surfaces.

Enamel paints available to model makers may be used to paint on ceramic or glass surfaces but the results tend to be quite thick and clumsy. Thinning the paints makes them easier to handle but more transparent. Enamel will chip off if the objects are handled.

Drawing out your design on paper and fastening it to the back of the object makes painting on glass easier.

No need to be an expert artist – naive painting looks great on a plate in strong colours.

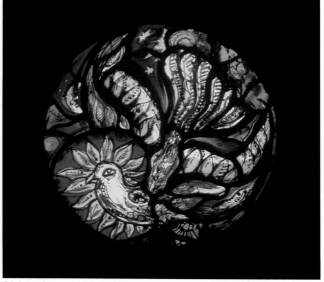

Using the paints on glass produces a vibrant stained window effect, so use your colours boldly.

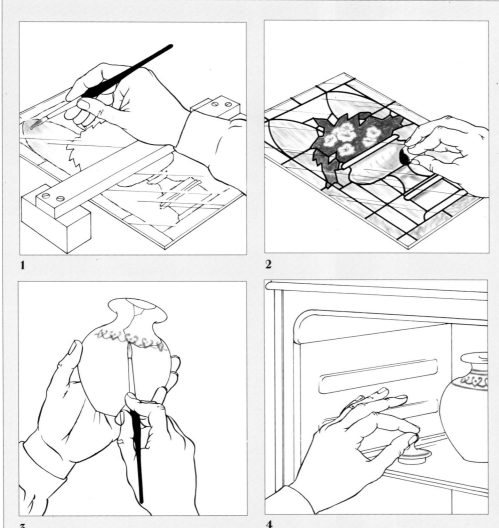

1 If you are painting a decoration on a flat piece of glass, lay the glass over the design. To avoid smearing the paint or moving the glass, you may find that it helps to use an armrest.

2 Imitation glass leading can be bought in rolls. Keep to a single colour within each outlined area and make sure that all the strips of false leading inter-connect, leading out to the edges of the picture.

3 Ceramic paints offer the chance to rescue broken china. Once the adhesive has set, gently smooth over the surface with fine sandpaper, then cover the cracks with a painted decoration.

4 Water-based ceramic paints must be set in an oven. It is wise to check before decorating the object that it will fit comfortably in your oven, without any painted part touching the oven or any other surface.

SPECIAL BACKGROUND FINISHES

Where you intend to have a painted surface beneath your design, you might like to try a special broken-paint effect. This can look particularly effective on a wall or on a piece of wooden furniture or panelling, where ragging, dragging or sponging will disguise a less-than-perfect surface or an indifferent timber. It is also a useful device for creating an old-fashioned appearance or linking one object to another visually. Furniture with doors or panels also lends itself to painting individual panels of background colour to combine a plain timber and painted effect.

Broken paint effects are applied using thinned household paint or tinted glazes on a flat-painted background – oil-based eggshell is a favourite soft sheen finish for this. Glazes can be shiny, matt or transparent. Transparent glaze is available from specialist paint suppliers and is tinted with stains or artists' oil colours. You can make your own glaze from one part linseed oil, one part turpentine, one part drying agent and a little colour. Alternatively, thin oil-based paint with white spirit.

The secret of success with most of these effects is to finish complete sections at a time, before the paint dries, so that you do not get any 'joins'. For this reason, slower drying paints are easier to use than fast drying water-based ones.

All the effects described are easy to attempt, but it is a good idea to have a spare piece of card at hand to practise until the stroke looks right; a simple twist or pressure of the hand can make all the difference and

it is a good idea to use your card or paper as a testing ground each time you reload your brush, sponge or rag. This avoids applying any mistakes directly onto your object. Most effects are remarkably quick to apply once you have applied your flat base colour and allowed it to dry for 24 hours. You can apply pale colours to a dark background and vice versa to equal effect. You should also allow your broken finish plenty of time to dry – at least three days – before starting your design. One word of warning over large areas: no two people apply such techniques in quite the same way so it is important you finish the job yourself. If you need to share the task, arrange it so that one of you applies the paint and the other the finish. It is a good tip to use a piece of card at any internal corners to prevent the paint blotching on the opposite surface.

Decorative painted panels

These are are an excellent device for positioning your designs on drawers and cupboard fronts. You must mark their position with chalk, taking care that they are centrally placed. Mask off the area with masking tape, if necessary, and paint in your panel in a contrasting or coordinating colour. You can remove the tape and reposition it to create borders where required, or incorporate decorative corners by painting in a freehand design, perhaps based on circles or triangles. Border details can be highlighted using a darker or lighter colour for a three-dimensional effect. Allow the paint to dry thoroughly before painting your central design.

You can let your imagination and paintbrush run wild with trompe l'oeil *effects.*

1 In dragging, an oil-based topcoat paint is thinned with ten parts paint to two parts white spirit and two parts scumble glaze (available from specialist paint suppliers) and applied evenly to the surface with a brush or roller. Before the thinned paint dries, take a clean, long-haired household paint brush and drag it firmly down in long continuous strokes to produce a lined effect.

2 Colour washing is one of the simplest paint effects. Emulsion paints are generally used, and when the base coat has dried, thin your chosen topcoat colour with water and apply it with a large brush in a random way to make an irregular coloured effect. Apply a second coat in the same way.

3 Stippling utilizes a special bristle stippling brush which looks rather like a gentleman's hairbrush. You must dab the brush lightly in your top-coat paint and apply it to the wall with a dabbing motion; work over a fairly large area to ensure that the paint is distributed evenly, as the brush will be more heavily loaded to begin with. Change the angle of the brush from time to time to keep the look irregular.

4 Rag rolling can be achieved with either oil- or water-based paints. Apply the base coat in the normal way. Prepare a thin glaze or wash; roll a cloth into a sausage shape; soak it in the glaze or wash, and then roll it down over the surface, changing direction and adjusting the cloth regularly.

1

2

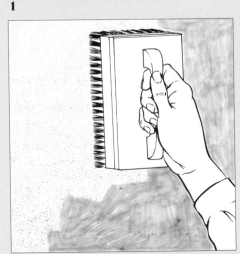

3

4

COLOUR MIXING

Acrylic paints are water-based and are therefore mixed with water – cheaper than specially formulated acrylic media gels or the oils and white spirit required by oil-based paints. Mixed with a little water, they produce the effect of oil paint; diluted with plenty of water, they can be used like a watercolour wash. Their big advantage is that they dry very quickly, which means several colours and effects can be applied during a single sitting. Used thinly, they have a transparent appearance but the addition of white will produce more of an opaqueness at the same time as it lightens the colours. Overpainting when the colours have dried is a useful technique to deepen colours or highlight areas, producing a subtly translucent effect in the manner of water-colour washes.

Colour mixing tips

Colour mixing is very much a case of trial and error, and it is worth experimenting until you achieve exactly the effect you want. Remember that fewer colours are better than too many and that it is better to mix your different shades from a limited palette to produce a sophisticated subtle effect.

White, as we have already mentioned, will make a colour lighter but also more opaque. Sometimes a pale lemon, light ochre or sienna produces a more subtle, antique effect. Yellow ochre or raw sienna is useful for lightening greens, or to give blues a lighter, turquoise tint.

Black should be used as little as possible as it has a deadening effect. Add raw umber or Payne's grey to your base to make up a darker shade for shadows.

Green is always a difficult colour to choose and tends to look rather artificial or synthetic. Hooker's green is always a good choice, lightened with white or yellow ochre or darkened with raw umber. Also try mixing yellow ochre and a brown to make a realistic green. Raw umber and turquoise produce a subtle green.

Reds also need careful choosing and the particular shade can be crucial if you want to achieve a certain colour. You must use crimson, for example, mixed with Monestial blue and maybe a touch of white to make a good purple or mauve. You need cadmium red to mix with cadmium yellow and white to make attractive coral pinks and apricots. Venetian red is useful under gold to achieve an antique effect: you can leave the red showing or rub off a little when dry.

Varnishing

Some colours like Hooker's green and Monestial blue (sometimes called phthalo blue) tend to run a bit when varnish is applied. Adding a little white paint when you mix the paint should help to overcome this problem. Oil-based gold paints also tend to run when varnished. Acrylic-based gold paint (like Plaka gold by Pelican) does not run and is more manageable.

Varnish comes in matt, eggshell or gloss finish. Two coats is generally sufficient unless you need a very tough finish. Remember that varnish has a yellowing effect over the years and that the more coats you apply, the more yellow the effect. For this reason, it is not a good idea to use plain white as your base coat.

Gloss varnish is tougher than matt, so if you need a highly resistant finish, you can apply a couple of coats of gloss, rub these down with fine sandpaper and then add on a final coat of matt varnish. Matt varnish does not normally need rubbing down between coats.

You should varnish the object as quickly as possible, a section at a time, spreading the varnish *thinly* from the centre in all directions, using the brush in a "flip flop" or slapping manner. If a speck of fluff or an insect drops into the varnish and you don't spot it straight away, it is better to leave it there until the varnish is dry before trying to remove it.

When a complete section has been covered in a thin coat of varnish, you should stroke the brush in a parallel motion against the grain. Finally, use the brush with the grain to finish off and avoid any obvious brush marks.

Varnish the next section as quickly as possible in the same way, overlapping a little. Check the surface against the light to make sure that it is completely covered.

When the whole piece is finished, you should go over it again with the brush, working with the grain to finish.

1 *Monestial blue (left) and cadmium yellow pale (right) make a leafy green. For a duller green, mix Monestial blue with yellow ochre.*

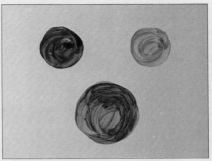

2 *Raw sienna (right) and turquoise (left) mix to a greeny brown (an extra touch of raw sienna adds to the brown effect).*

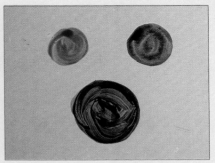

3 *Instead of adding black, red can be mixed with green to darken it; here, Venetian red (left) is used to darken Hooker's green (right).*

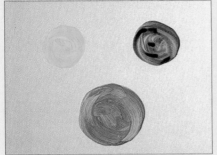

4 *Yellow can be used to lighten a green; here, cadmium yellow deep (left) is added to Hooker's green (right).*

5 *The addition of white to Hooker's green will produce a less grassy green.*

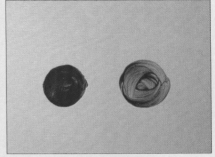

6 *Acrylic medium can be used to achieve extra translucency without thinning; here, cadmium red light (left) is mixed with acrylic medium.*

7 *Lightening or shading blue, reading from the top down to the left, straight down, then down to the right: Monestial blue can be mixed with Payne's grey to give a cold, night sky shadow; mixed with white, the result is a soft, light blue; mixed with raw umber, the result is a much warmer shading colour than the grey blue.*

8 *Cadmium red light lightened and shaded, reading from the top down to the left, straight down, then down to the right: the addition of burnt umber creates a warm, brick red shade; white gives a pinkish highlight colour; mixed with Payne's grey, the result is a cold shadow.*

9 *Different reds and blues can be used to mix a varying range of purples. Reading from the top down to the left, straight down, then down to the right: crimson (top) mixed with Monestial blue makes a dull, purple; mixed with white only, the result is a pink highlight colour; mixed with ultramarine, the resulting purple is much richer than the first.*

CHAPTER THREE

ABSTRACT DESIGNS

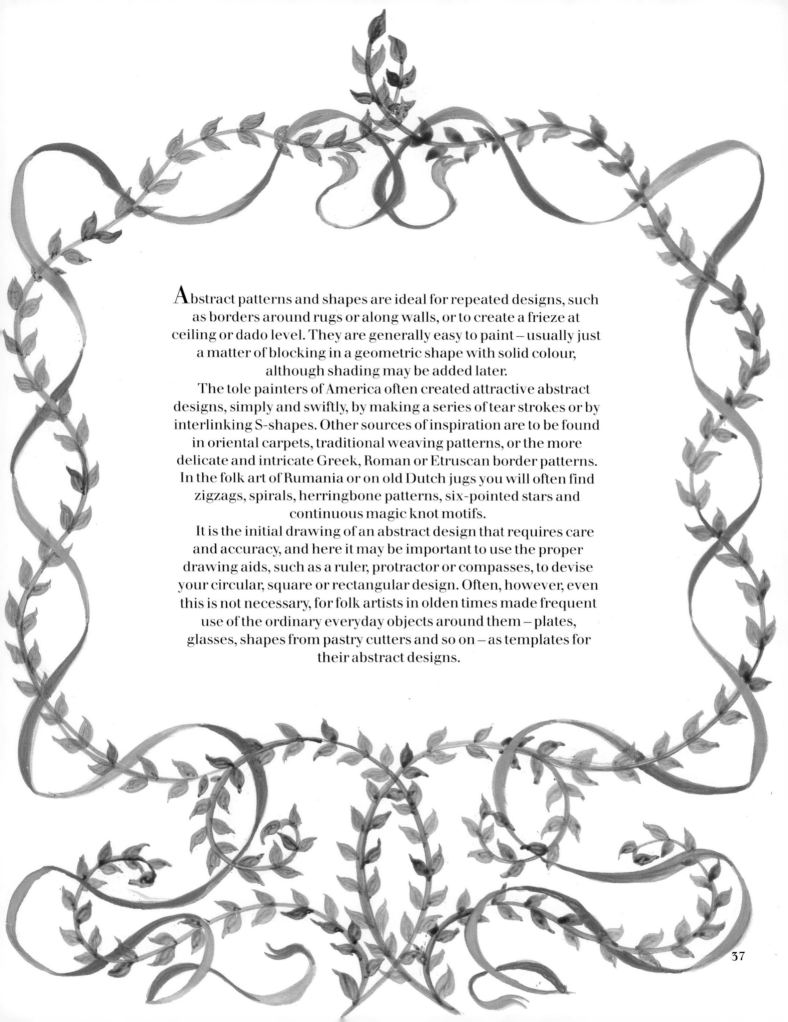

Abstract patterns and shapes are ideal for repeated designs, such as borders around rugs or along walls, or to create a frieze at ceiling or dado level. They are generally easy to paint – usually just a matter of blocking in a geometric shape with solid colour, although shading may be added later.

The tole painters of America often created attractive abstract designs, simply and swiftly, by making a series of tear strokes or by interlinking S-shapes. Other sources of inspiration are to be found in oriental carpets, traditional weaving patterns, or the more delicate and intricate Greek, Roman or Etruscan border patterns. In the folk art of Rumania or on old Dutch jugs you will often find zigzags, spirals, herringbone patterns, six-pointed stars and continuous magic knot motifs.

It is the initial drawing of an abstract design that requires care and accuracy, and here it may be important to use the proper drawing aids, such as a ruler, protractor or compasses, to devise your circular, square or rectangular design. Often, however, even this is not necessary, for folk artists in olden times made frequent use of the ordinary everyday objects around them – plates, glasses, shapes from pastry cutters and so on – as templates for their abstract designs.

DECORATIVE EGGS

Painted eggs are a good project for the beginner: they are small and easy to handle; they offer quick results, and they make excellent presents or ornaments. Because neither real, nor papier mâché nor wooden eggs are expensive, and you need very little paint, you can afford to experiment – why not make a whole collection of different designs? Strong colours and simple patterns produce a feeling reminiscent of East European folk art, and once they have been highly varnished the eggs look almost like jewels. Wooden and papier maché eggs are readily available from craft and gift shops and are easier to handle than real eggs, which must be pierced and have their insides blown out.

Before you start to decorate an egg, you must first seal the surface with an acrylic primer or layer of undercoat; the acrylic is better because it dries more quickly. Apply the primer by holding the top and bottom of the egg between your finger and thumb and paint as much of the egg as possible, almost in a saddle shape. Put it down carefully to dry, then hold the 'saddle' while you paint the remaining areas. Next you must paint on your base colour in eggshell or silk vinyl paint (the eggshell is preferable), holding the egg in exactly the same way between your finger and thumb. The base colour of the pink egg was a pale pink silk vinyl; for the blue and green egg, a pale beige; and for the gold egg, pale coffee.

RED & PINK EGG

S T E P   1

This is the most rudimentary of our egg designs and involves a circle drawn as a starting point around the rounded end of the egg using a pencil or a waterproof black pen with a fine nib. The pattern of petals is subsequently based on a simple rounded shape. From the small circle, ringing the end of the egg, draw four equidistant petals like scallops or loops. To these you must add your next row of petals, putting two petals onto each one of the previous shapes as the egg starts to get a little wider. For succeeding rows, draw in the same number of petals each time, but make them slightly larger until you reach the widest point and then smaller as required by the tapering shape of the egg. The petals of each round should be spaced with the points falling in between the petals of the row above. When you reach the bottom of the egg, go back and elongate your petals slightly to make them more leaf shaped – a slightly more pointed end should give the right effect.

S T E P   2

Using crimson acrylic paint, paint over all the drawn lines using a fine artists' brush – no. 1 or 2.

S T E P   3

The same brush and colour are then used to mark in a few small vertical lines on each petal, with none of the

lines touching the outside edge, so as to suggest the convex shape of a petal.

S T E P   4

This egg was given two coats of gloss varnish, tinted with a little Venetian red to tone down the pink, which contrasted too strongly at first with the background. You can tint any varnish with artists' oil

paint if you first mix the paint with a little turpentine or white spirit and then pour the varnish onto it.

BLUE & GREEN EGG

STEP 1

The petals are drawn in the same way as for the pink egg, starting with the small circle. Three strong colours were chosen for this pattern: turquoise, blue and green. The turquoise colour is painted first, covering not quite every other leaf shape but in a random arrangement to ensure that no turquoise petals were touching each other.

STEP 2

The second colour, blue, is applied close to the first, again making sure that no two adjacent leaves have the same colour.

STEP 3

Most of the remaining leaves are completed in the third colour, green.

STEP 4

This still leaves some blanks, so the turquoise and green are mixed to provide a complementary fourth colour for the remaining leaf shapes.

STEP 5

Shading will add richness and depth to your design. Here, a mixture of the blue and green paints is used to put a simple line of shading beneath each leaf shape at the point where it overlaps the leaf below.

STEP 6

With a larger, medium-sized waterproof black pen, the central stem and ribs are drawn in on each shape, but not quite to the edges so as to accentuate the impression of leaves. When the egg is finished, give it a couple of coats of polyurethane gloss varnish to make it more durable and jewel-like.

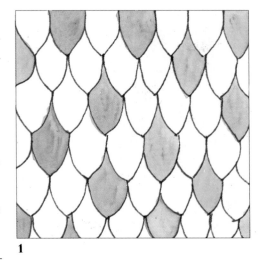

1

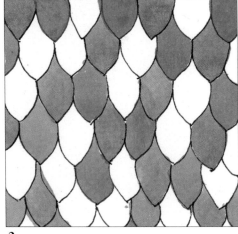

2

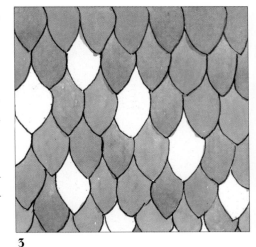

3

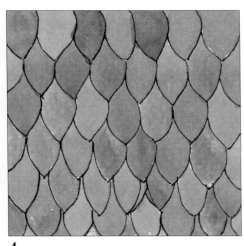

4

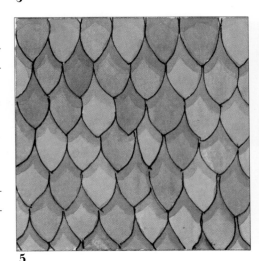

5

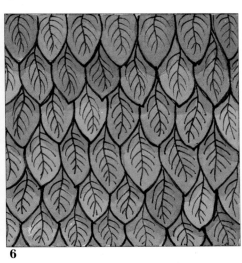

6

BLACK & GOLD EGG

STEP 1

Like the pink egg, this begins with a circle at one end, drawn either with a pencil or a waterproof pen with a fine nib. The repeated pattern is again based on a series of loops or circles, but this time they are flattened into a sort of 'S' shape like a Spanish tile. When the design has been expanded and contracted to fit the shape of the egg and the bottom has been reached, each shape is divided in half with a vertical line.

STEP 2

One half of each shape is painted black. Keep the same half throughout the design: in this case, the right-hand half.

STEP 3

The other, left-hand side of each shape, is painted gold. Acrylic gold paint is used and a small gold dot placed in the centre of each black section. A painted dot is made by loading a small brush with paint so that you almost, but not quite, get a drip on the end – you should use a small brush with a tapered end for this. Let the paint on the end of your brush slide gently into position to make a dot exactly where you need it.

STEP 4

For the final effect, use artists' acrylic paint in burnt umber, putting a puddle of this on a plate. Paint a line of burnt umber down the centre of each shape, dividing black from gold. The burnt umber should be feathered slightly into the gold, creating an impressive harlequin design. As before, the egg should be finished with a couple of coats of gloss varnish.

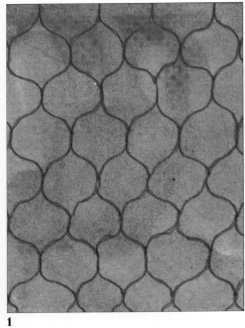

1

2

3

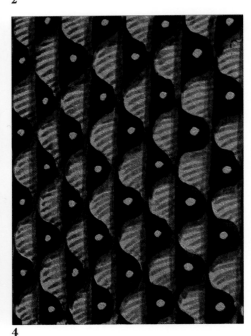

4

FRAME WITH RIBBONS AND FRONDS

A hand-decorated picture or mirror frame can look very stylish, especially if it coordinates with your paint or paper, or has been designed to suit a particular print or painting. You can create a brightly patterned effect or, as on the mirror frame shown here, a three-dimensional impression of hand carving, with the luxurious addition of a little gold paint. Buy or make your frame or restore an old one; these can often be picked up cheaply if the picture within is rather dreadful.

We took a plain pine mirror frame and gave it a coat of water-based acrylic primer, followed by a layer of undercoat. Between coats, we rubbed the surface gently with sandpaper to make sure that it was smooth. Next, we applied a coat of coffee-coloured eggshell paint; this was thinly brushed out so that the white undercoat would show through and give an antique effect. Before the paint was dry, we dragged the brush lightly along the grain.

This dragged finish was allowed to dry overnight and was then rubbed gently all over with very fine sandpaper to key the surface for acrylic paint.

When the design has been completed, the frame can be antiqued, as described for the Antiqued Paeony Cupboard. Before the mixture has dried, use kitchen paper to remove most of it, wiping gently and taking more of the mixture off those areas that would be most faded. Follow the grain of the wood and try to keep the effect even. Wrap a little paper around your index finger and run it along the lines of gold dots to highlight them. When you are satisfied with the effect (if you are not, you can always wipe the mixture off and start afresh), leave the frame to dry and then finish it with a coat of varnish. A matt varnish is best, as gloss tends to be too hard for an antique effect. Over a matt varnish you can, if you leave the frame for two or three weeks, add a last finishing touch in the form of a coat of tinted wax.

TWO-COLOUR PAINTING: ROUND-ENDED BRUSH

The leaves in this design are painted in two colours at once, using a round-ended brush. The result of this technique, which is found in Norwegian *Rosemaling*, is a three-dimensional effect. To paint the leaves of this design, mix two separate puddles of paint on your plate, one of raw sienna and one of burnt umber, making sure that the paint is not too runny.

Rinse out the brush, then load one side with raw sienna and the other with burnt umber. Twist the brush on its side and make simple tear-shaped brush strokes, one for each leaf.

After a while, the brush will get clogged and you will start to lose the two-tone effect, so about a quarter of the way around it is wise to rinse the brush out and repeat the loading process. You can, of course, use any two colours, but two close shades produces a soft and delightfully subtle impression.

STEP 1

To mark out the pattern, first measure your frame, finding the length and width as measured from a point halfway between the inner and outer edges of the frame. Decide how many sections of the design will fall comfortably into these measurements and mark the divisions on the frame: in the case of the frame shown here, the sections were 6.5cm (2½in), with sections of a slightly smaller size – 3.8cm (1½in) – at the corners. It is best to find and mark the centre point on each side of the frame and to mark out from these points rather than starting from the corners.

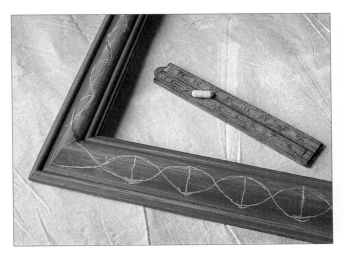

STEP 2

Imagining the design to be centred on a line (not drawn) running all around the frame, halfway between the inner and outer edges, draw two arcs in each section, one falling below the imaginary centre line and one above it. You now effectively have two wavy lines running around the frame and crossing at each marked intersection. Choose one line for the branch and one for the ribbon.

STEP 3

Start by painting the branch line, using burnt umber and a touch of raw sienna, mixed with a little water on a plate and applied with a fairly small – no. 2 – brush. Paint the wavy line all around the frame and then paint the leaves, using the two-colour technique, as shown. Paint the leaves in pairs, all the way along the branch, leaving a gap at each intersection where the branch crosses with the ribbon.

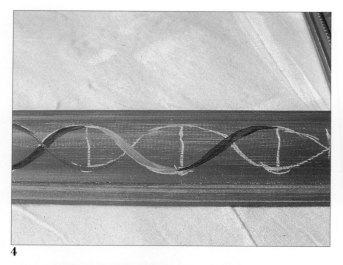

4

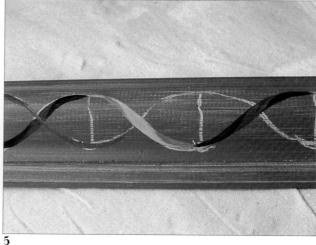

5

6

7

STEP 4

When the leaves are finished, paint in the ribbon. Bear in mind that where it slipped behind the branch it would be in shadow and that where it was twined in front it would be highlighted, and accentuate the effect by using plain burnt umber for the ribbon behind and raw sienna and a little white for the ribbon in front. To show the effect more clearly we have illustrated a section where the leaves have not yet been painted.

Start painting at the apex of the arc, using the tip of the brush to produce a thin starting point. By pressing down when you reach the middle of each section, you will fatten the line; lift the brush up again as you move towards the apex of the next arc. This produces a flattened-out S-shape for both dark and light parts.

STEP 5

When both the light and dark sections of the ribbon have dried, highlight the centre section of the light one with an even lighter shade. The darkest corners of the back one are given a second coat of burnt umber to darken them. The picture shows the ribbon only, for clarity.

STEP 6

The completed leaves and ribbon together: wait until the paint has dried completely before rubbing away any remaining chalk marks.

STEP 7

For an extra special effect, we touched in the leaves with gold paint, using a type with an acrylic base. This is easier to handle than other gold paints and doesn't run when you apply an oil-based varnish. To add the gold, use a very small brush (no. 0 or 1) and highlight each leaf, working on the theory that the light is coming from one corner – we chose the top left-hand corner, so all the left and top sides were picked out with a fine gold line. We wanted to accentuate the rounded moulding on the inside of the frame but painting a straight line on a curve is quite difficult so we decided instead to paint a row of dots. This is much easier and is equally effective. To paint the dots, load the brush with a fair amount of paint – the point is not to brush the paint into a circle but to blob a little paint into a blot. Paint all the dots by eye, leaving very small gaps between them, right around the inside and outside of the design.

NEW LAMPS FOR OLD – SPONGED CERAMICS

Ceramic lamp bases are expensive home accessories, particularly if you want them to match your other decorations. When you change your scheme, the lamp shade is relatively easy and not too expensive to replace, but a new base can be a drain on a tight budget. Painting your existing lamp base will not only save you this expense, but will also produce exactly the design and colour that you need for a highly original effect. This base was a bright lime green, a colour that no longer fitted the surrounding décor, but we liked the shape and were willing to try a change to a more suitable finish.

Water-based ceramic paints were used. These are easy to use and, after the item has been baked in the oven for half an hour, perfectly durable. This lamp was fired twice – once after sponging and again after the 'S' shapes were painted on. It is important to remove the wiring before you paint in the design, because these paints must be proved by cooking the painted item in a domestic oven according to the manufacturer's instructions. In this case, the oven was first heated to 200°C for 15 minutes, then lowered to 150°C and the object baked on its side for half an hour.

TWO COLOUR PAINTING: SQUARE-ENDED BRUSH

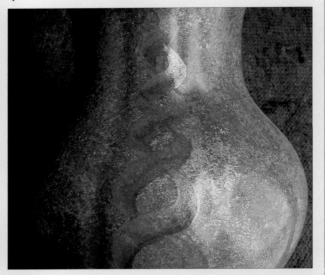

Using ceramic paint, mix up two puddles of paint; in this case, one is mostly white with gold powder sprinkled on, and the other an emerald colour. Dipping the brush sideways into the first (gold) mixture, load about two-thirds of the brush with paint. Turn it over and dip the other third into the second (emerald) colour.

When you use a square-tipped oil-painting brush – about 1.3cm (½in) long and 0.6cm (¼in) wide – like an italic pen, a sideways action will produce a thin stroke, and by turning the brush straight so that the full width of the tip is used, you can make a fat stroke. We use this technique to produce a twisted rope or ribbon.

S T E P 1

An all over sponged effect
tones well with a more
modern decorative
scheme and the preferred
colour, which in this
instance is a blue green. To
achieve this, the lamp base
is first painted bright blue
and then sponged, before
the first paint is dry. To do
this, a natural sponge
(never use a synthetic one)
is rinsed in water and
squeezed almost dry, and
is then pressed or pounced
lightly onto the wet
surface in a random
manner, removing some of
the paint to create a soft
cloud-like impression.
When the paint is dry, the
effect can be examined
and adjusted, where
necessary, by applying a
little paint to the damp
sponge with a brush and
then sponging in any
spaces that look too light.

S T E P 2

When this has dried, the
next colour can be applied
– in this case, emerald
green and white mixed
half and half. This shade is
applied in cloud-like
patches, by putting the
paint on the sponge with
the brush, as before, and
then sponging it onto the
lamp. If you tried to sponge
the second colour directly
onto the lamp you would
damage the first colour.
This is also why it is
necessary to prove the
object twice between
decorating the base and
applying the decoration.
Use the sponge to apply
the second colour in a
random diagonal motion,
leaving patches of the
original blue showing.

S T E P 3

The final brilliant touch is added to the background by sprinkling a little bronze powder into the white mixture and, using the sponge, dabbing a few clouds of this onto the existing white patches: a simple way to create a wonderfully sophisticated effect. The lamp base is then proved for the first time, as described.

S T E P 4

With gold and emerald green on the square-tipped brush, as described in the technique section, paint a series of continuous 'S' shapes vertically down the lamp base, then prove it in the oven for the second time.

Imagining the light to come from the top left-hand corner, we made sure that the emerald green was on the bottom of our brush, and the gold on the top. The finished lamp base looks like beautiful lustre-ware, but the design is basically very simple and can be applied with the minimum of effort.

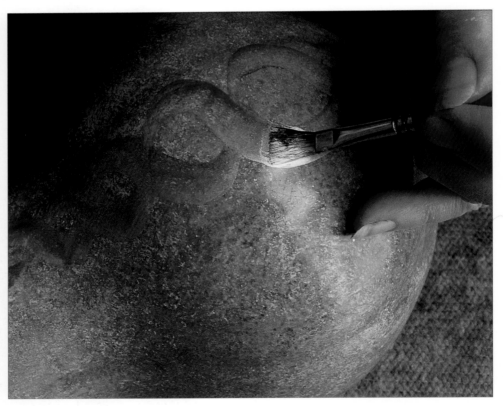

HAND-PAINTED WALL FRIEZE

A hand-painted frieze is an excellent way to enliven a dull wall or create visual illusions. You can, for example, use it to lower a ceiling that is visually too high, or, at dado height, to lengthen a short expanse of wall space, choosing colours to coordinate with your general decorative scheme.

Here we have chosen a simple shape – a heart – and inverted it, then embellished it with light touches of the brush to produce an ornate finish. Getting the shaded three-dimensional effect can be tricky to begin with, but once the first shape is right, the rest follow easily and look remarkably good.

Begin by deciding at what level you want your pattern to run; either just below the ceiling, above the picture rail, or at dado (chair rail) height. Check that your design is not likely to be obscured by a piece of furniture and, if possible, take your lead from some other feature in the room, such as a picture rail.

A chalk line is essential to plot the position of your frieze and to draw this you will need a spirit level, a long rule, a piece of blackboard chalk and, if possible, a friend to help you. Measure down from the ceiling, adding a little to the intended depth of the frieze to allow for adjustments. For a frieze at dado height, measure up from the floor. Mark a series of points along the wall, then join these points with a ruler. Check with your spirit level that they are horizontally aligned, making adjustments if necessary. For a vertical line, use a plumb bob, or some other point of reference in the room. We used the window frame as our point of reference but do not rely on doors or windows to be true and always double check with your spirit level.

Once you have your line, decide what size you want your design to be. It helps to rough in one or two of your pattern repeats then stand back and view them from a distance to see what sort of effect they achieve. We began with a pattern 13cm (5in) square; this looked fine close to, but was rather too large seen from a distance, so we scaled it down to 10cm (4in).

KEYING A PAINTED SURFACE

If you are using acrylic or water-based paint on a wall that has been painted with an oil-based eggshell or silk vinyl base colour, you may find that your design goes a little bobbly where the water won't take to the oil. To avoid this, rub the surface gently with very fine sandpaper or flourpaper before painting your design. You should have no problems if the wall has been emulsioned, but because emulsion is more absorbent, your design will have a fuzzier, less crisp appearance. Test your paint on the wall before you begin, wiping off with a damp cloth before it dries.

Another way to ensure that water-based paint does not bubble or peel is to add a drop or two of soft washing-up liquid when mixing the paint on your plate.

S T E P 1

To plot the design, start by making the pattern guide out of thin cardboard. The guide is cut to the maximum height and width of the shape. Measure in 1.2cm (½in) from the left-hand side and draw a vertical line: this will act as a spacer between shapes. Next, draw a vertical centre line down the template, then parallel lines to either side to indicate the distance between the matching loops at the bottom of the design. The horizontal line marks the maximum height of the inner loops. To use the template, butt it up to the preceding shape and use the left-hand spacer line to mark a 1.2cm (½in) gap between this and the shape you are about to draw. Move the template along the wall to the marked points, then put in the other registration marks (three at the top, three at the bottom and one at each side).

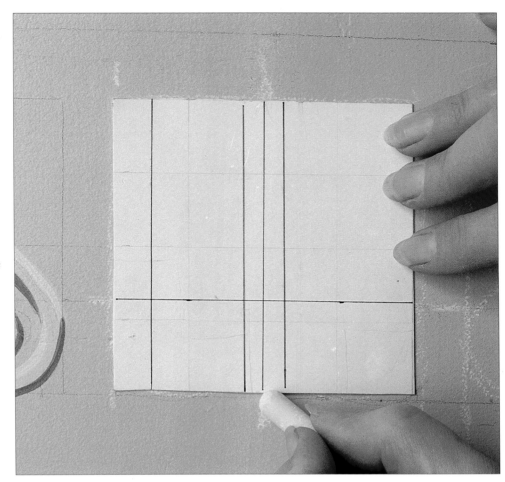

S T E P 2

These marks are joined with straight lines to provide the guide for drawing. The chalk outline of the heart can be drawn freehand, though you could use a flexible curve. In fact, however, it is much easier to work freehand than you may imagine: remember that you are only working with a repeated series of curves. If the design does not look quite right, the beauty of chalk is that you can always rub it out and start again.

STEP 3

When your design is drawn in, you can start painting. Here we used a no. 8 watercolour brush. This may seem rather large, but it will help you to produce a good strong stroke if you use a slightly larger brush than you think you need. You will have to make fewer strokes and this will produce a more successful freehand effect; a smaller brush would encourage you to draw a thin outline and then fill it in.

Start with the main shape – in this case, the inverted heart – then add the loops and, lastly, the teardrop strokes, of which there are five. Make a little dot at the top of the heart, then turn your brush upside down to paint the point at the top. Each stroke should be a separate pass of the brush, a technique you will soon find easy to repeat as you move along your pattern.

At this stage, the pattern looks quite light and transparent – we were using a beige paint on a terracotta red base colour. Don't worry if the design looks lightweight: once you have added the shadows and highlights it will strengthen.

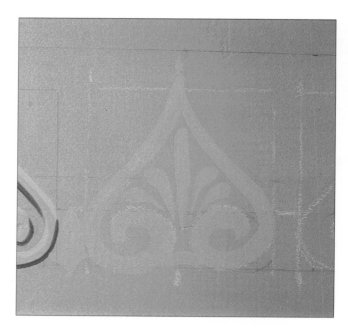

STEP 4

You should next put in the shadows. Use a smaller brush for this – here we used a no. 4. Where we had used household paint for the main colour, for the shadows and highlights we used artists' acrylics; in this case, a burnt umber mixed with a little white. This is mixed up on an old plate to a creamy consistency so that it slips easily off the brush without dribbling. Getting the shadows in the right position to suggest the fall of light may take a little practice, but once you have the first shape right the rest should be easy. The secret is to imagine your design carved in stone. Decide where the light is coming from – here we decided it was from a window, at the top left-hand corner. Thus the shadows fall on the right hand side and below the design. Where the shadow would peter out, we brought the line to a point and faded it away.

STEP 5

When you have put in all the shadows and are happy with the effect, plot in your highlights. For this, use the no. 4 brush again and a lighter shade of your main colour. Because ours was a fairly light colour to begin with, we used white acrylic for our highlights. The overall painting should consist of approximately one third main colour, one third shadow and one third highlight. Select your highlighting as you did your shadows by imagining how the light would fall on a three-dimensional design.

Now stand back and appraise your design: if you feel the shadows are too hard, soften the colour with more white and repaint where necessary.

KILIM-STYLE FLOOR RUG

A piece of painted canvas can make an excellent and surprisingly durable rug. This is one of those clever and thrifty crafts originally devised by New England settlers and currently enjoying a revival of interest among today's more imaginative interior designers. The technique is easy and lends itself to abstract designs based on a series of parallel borders or repeated goemetric shapes. The most important stage of the work is making the templates, which must be drawn accurately.

We used a piece of thick cotton canvas, bought from an art shop. This type of canvas comes in generous widths and is available in a range of coarse and fine finishes. To prepare the canvas for the decorative painting, start by giving it from three to four coats of acrylic gesso: this will give it body and seal the fibres. The gesso is rather dry and you will find that it helps if you water down the first coat.

The canvas must be stretched taut while you are painting it or it will ruck and rumple. We stapled ours to the top of a large plan chest, but you could attach yours to a frame or even – if the weather is fine – peg it out on the lawn in the garden and work outside. The canvas will tend to shrink a little, so position your pegs or staples well outside the pattern area and remember to allow a turning of between 5cm (2in) and 7.5cm (3in) on all sides so that the edges of the finished rug can be turned under.

To prevent the finished rug from cracking and to give it some protection from everyday wear and tear, it should be given several coats of varnish and some form of padding or underlay – such as a second layer of canvas – underneath. Fasten the rug to the floor with double-sided rug tape, to prevent it slipping.

If you have to store the finished rug for any reason, always roll it up; never fold it or it will tend to crack.

WOVEN TEXTILE EFFECT

You can reproduce the effect of woven wool or textiles when painting a fake tapestry or rug by allowing the colour to come and go a little and keeping the brush moving in the same direction across the grain. You need a no. 8 or 9 square-ended hog's hair brush and a fairly runny mixture of paint. The colour is stroked on keeping the grain going crossways to imitate the movement of the loom and allowing it to thin a little as the brush begins to run out of paint. You can emphasize this effect by thinning the paint slightly with water to produce a patchy, faded, worn effect. The colours should be merged slightly when wet to avoid any hard lines.

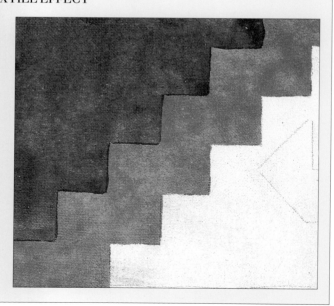

S T E P   1

The pattern is based on a Turkish rug design and incorporates a few stylized animal motifs. Using a long ruler and a soft pencil, begin by drawing central registration lines from top to bottom and side to side, to find the centre of the rug. Next, draw the outer edges of the design, remembering to leave an even turning all around. Then draw a second border line, 2.5cm (1in) in from the outer edge. The design is based on 2.5cm (1in) squares and it is easy when using the templates to make the squares just a little larger each time, so that the design becomes distorted and you run out of space: to avoid this, mark off the inner border lines in 2.5cm (1in) divisions.

Using the pencil and template 1 and starting at the centre point on one side, start marking the border pattern. The template is used first one way (with the 'legs' meeting the inner border line) and is then reversed (so that the 'head' meets the inner border line) to create an interlocking design. Work out to one corner, then go back to the centre point and work out to the other corner. Complete all the sides in the same way.

S T E P   2

Use template 2 to draw the three big square panels that are positioned at an angle to the outer edges and are the focal points of the design. The template has eight steps and you will see that there are 15 steps in a complete square, so draw in one half of a square and then keep the bottom level of the template in the same place when you flip it over to draw the second half, otherwise you will have a double-width section at the centre. When you have completed these squares, draw the smaller squares in the same way, but only using six of the steps. Complete the large squares by using template 3 to draw in the central motifs (the legs and other details are filled in freehand).

The process of drawing the design on the canvas is rather like building up a crossword, and it helps to use the graph drawing as a guide throughout.

STEP 3

When you have drawn the entire design, start painting, working with the grain of the canvas in order to create a woven fabric effect.

We used PVA paint, which is fairly runny, but you could also use acrylic paints. The brush used here was a no. 10 fine quality oil-paint brush, made of hog's hair and filbert-ended, but it would have been equally possible to use a no. 8 or 9 square-ended hog's hair brush. We blocked in the colours, merging different shades of the same basic colour while the paint was still wet, to avoid hard dividing lines.

Start with the border, filling in the cream first and then using two slightly different shades of brown to achieve a pleasantly worn, patchy effect: start with burnt umber; after you have filled in about 60cm (2ft) add a little burnt sienna, then return to plain burnt umber after about another 30cm (1ft). When you have finished the border, paint the blue background, followed by the red areas, then fill in the background and motifs of the squares.

STEP 4

When all the paint has dried, varnish the rug. Although gloss is the most hard-wearing varnish it produces a glazed, linoleum-like effect. Matt looks better but is not as tough, so soft sheeny eggshell is perhaps the best compromise (an alternative would be to apply two coats of gloss, followed by two coats of matt). A minimum of four coats will be needed for protection. You can add a touch of Venetian red oil paint to the varnish to produce a mellowed effect.

When the varnish has dried, you can remove the pegs or staples and turn the edges under. Be careful to get this right first time as the canvas will crack when you crease it. Fasten down the turnings and attach any underlay with PVA-based glue.

FLORAL THEMES

Finished flowers may look quite complicated, but they are really only made up of various standard brush strokes: simple tear drop, petal and leaf strokes, dots and circles, with the clever addition of highlight and shadow shades to create a three-dimensional effect. With only limited experience of these brush strokes, it is possible to paint realistic daisies, roses, tulips, lilies and foliage. These can be combined to make self-contained rosettes or linked with foliage to create garlands which can be useful for borders. Garlands and rosettes of flowers are the most commonly seen motifs in folk art. For the Pennsylvanian Dutch, stylized brush strokes were more important than a realistic effect, a technique similar to that of the canal boatmen, who used bright brush strokes to create simple but effective roses, daisies and pansies.

The Norwegian flower painting or *Rosemaling* (begun around 1750) produces a far more sophisticated type of flower, often painted with two colours on the one brush, for a subtly shaded effect. A lot of the later, more detailed American and English floral furniture decoration was in imitation of Adam and Sheraton who decorated panels with wreaths of flowers.

If you like flowers, you can repeat a floral motif or garland, running it around the room as a frieze, or use it to decorate fabrics, furniture, ceramics or tinware.

ROSES AND DAISIES – BREAD BIN

A large tin bread bin is an excellent subject for hand decoration: it is a good size, easy to handle and usually rather a dull item on the shelf. You can paint a tin to match your kitchen decorations or to complement other storage containers and brighten up your kitchen or pantry. For the base colour of this tin, we used a special enamel paint with a hammered metal finish. This paint will save you a great deal of time and trouble when you decorate large items, for it hides any imperfections and will cover the surface evenly in one coat. The bin shown here was an old one, originally green with black handles, and the aim was to transform it with the minimum of effort into something brighter and more fun.

PAINTING ROSES

On a dark background, the roses are blocked in firstly with white. A simple ball shape is painted using white acrylic paint. A series of smaller circles round the main ball shape creates the petals. While the paint is still wet, the brush is used to re-accentuate the centre ball shape using a circular brush stroke motion. When the white has dried, the deep yellow acrylic is added to the central ball shape, keeping the brush strokes circular. The yellow petals are painted in, taking care not to obscure the centre painting. Using raw sienna the rose is shaded on the side away from the

imagined light source – in this case, the top left-hand corner. Shadows fall round each petal and from the centre of the main ball. The centre is marked in with this colour using a dab of the

brush. The same shadows are accentuated in the creases with a mixture of raw sienna and burnt umber. White highlight strokes are added on the opposite side from the shadows, where the imagined light would catch the flower.

PAINTING DAISIES

Begin with a single tear stroke using white paint to make the first petal. The brush starts at the fattest part of the petal and flicks in a single movement towards the tail. A second tear stroke

(petal) is painted, facing out from the first. A further four petals are added on the side closest to you using the same tear stroke technique. On the far side, four fore-shortened petals are

stroked in to give the correct perspective. When the paint is dry, the petals can be highlighted with more white, keeping the same

direction of brush stroke and imagining how the light would catch the petals if coming from the top left-hand side. The centre is filled in with yellow and shaded on the right side with raw sienna.

1

2

3

4

STEP 1

First find an object of a suitable size and shape to make a template: we found an oval dish that was ideal for the purpose. If your tin has a curved surface, it will not be possible to use the dish itself as a template, so the shape must be transferred to a pliable piece of card. Draw vertical and horizontal lines across the shape to mark the centre points. The tin can meanwhile be given a coat of enamel and allowed to dry.

STEP 2

Using the template, the oval outline is drawn on the bin in chalk. We felt that the design would be more attractive if some elements of the floral design were to overlap the oval, to create a freer and less stilted effect, so a rose is sketched in, again with chalk, at one side of the centre mark at the top of the oval; and a daisy is drawn at the other side, with a couple of trailing leaves in attendance. This arrangement is repeated at the other centre points around the oval and the flowers can then be linked with simple leaves. These are best drawn in chalk because although this is relatively difficult to see, it can easily be rubbed away afterwards. (A silver pen was used in the picture only because it would show up better in the photographs.)

STEP 3

Because the design is painted in a light colour against a dark background, it is first blocked in with plain white to ensure that the colours will show up correctly. White acrylic paint is used because it dries so quickly. As soon as this has dried, it is possible to go over the design in the chosen colours; in this case the daisies only really need highlighting. They are simply painted using single tear strokes, and the roses are painted in colour.

STEP 4

Next, the leaves and stalks are painted green, using flat brush strokes. The ears of corn are simply bobbles of yellow ochre, designed to give the impression of individual ears. To get that three-dimensional effect, the paint is applied generously with a fine pointed brush so that each blob of paint slides easily into position. You should aim to take just enough paint so that it will run to the tip of the brush (but no further!). When the main flowers and leaves are dry, the stems and leaves can be accented. Blue and green paint are mixed and used to suggest the veining (care must be taken not to go right to the edges). Half of each leaf is painted with the darker colour (it doesn't matter which half) to make the shadow and create a three-dimensional effect.

5

6

7

8

S T E P   5

When all the flowers and foliage are dry, the lettering can be added. Again, it is essential to plan the position of each letter in advance if the finished effect is to look even. You must first assess exactly how much space you have and divide the number of letters into it, allowing two extra spaces for breathing space at either end. Chalk in the sections as accurately as possible, then write the letters in chalk, adjusting them if necessary. Start in the centre and work out towards the sides.

S T E P   6

Over this rough outline, the letters are painted in plain white acrylic, pressing the brush down on the curves to allow the brush strokes to go a little wider on the rounded parts of each letter.

S T E P   7

The final stage is to add the gold lining. This is done to highlight the oval and the position of the gold line is determined by the original chalk line, now half-covered in leaves and flowers. A steady hand and a loaded brush produce a reasonably good line. The second line just inside the first has to be drawn by eye; this is not difficult providing you keep reasonably close to the original line. All that is necessary is to look ahead to the point where the brush is going. The lettering is also outlined in gold paint.

S T E P   8

The lid can be painted with a circular design of leaves and flowers to match but you can leave it plain if you prefer. As this is a very utilitarian item the whole bin should be given two coats of poly-urethane gloss varnish to produce a very hard-wearing durable piece.

ROSES AND DAISIES – COOKIE JAR

Marking your glass storage jars with a waterproof pen or sticky label is essential if you are to keep track of the contents, so why not try your hand at a little decorating at the same time? Decorated glass jars are expensive but plain ones are relatively cheap and are more readily available, either new or second hand. With hand painting as easy as this, you can start a collection to match your kitchen. This cookie jar was designed to match the bread bin; because of the thickness of the glass, it is difficult to be exact with your painting, but that of course, is half its charm.

For the painting, special oil-based ceramic paints were used; these were of a type recommended for use on glass and are formulated to produce a lighter, more opaque effect than model makers' enamels. These oil-based ceramic paints tend to be rather runny and take a long time to dry, so always work from the side that is opposite to the hand you use for painting. Using the method shown below, a whole series of matching jars can be painted with the minimum of effort, providing new lettering is marked in for the contents of each jar.

1

2

3

4

S T E P 1

It is difficult to draw on glass with something that will rub off easily afterwards, so an inner card pattern is used. First, measure your jar from the bottom to the point at which it begins to bend towards the neck. The inner circumference of the jar should also be measured and a piece of card cut to these two measurements.

The oval template used for the bread bin can also be used to mark in an oval shape in the centre of the card. Using a thin black pen, the complete design is plotted onto the card

pattern, which can be laid flat while this is done. The flowers and foliage are overlapped and the lettering spaced, as described for the Bread Bin.

The card template can then be rolled, design side out, and fitted inside the jar to show where the pattern is to be painted. The glass will distort the design a little but it does not take long to learn to adjust to this.

S T E P 2

The design is worked in the same way as for the bread bin using the pattern inside as a guide

and omitting any background painting. The paints are applied with quite a small brush, for this is reasonably delicate work, and colours are carefully mixed to get the right shadow shade. If you haven't got the exact shades that you need, experiment with mixing colours: this way you can work with a limited and therefore less expensive palette. If a colour is not sufficiently opaque, add a little white.

S T E P 3

Leaves are detailed with veining as follows: block the leaves in with flat

colour and then, while the paint is still wet, draw across the paint, taking the brush just a little beyond the edge of the leaves to produce the three-dimensional, quilted effect of veining, and at the same time the slightly serrated outline of a typical rose leaf.

S T E P 4

The letters are painted in white. On its own, white doesn't show up enough against the clear glass, so the letters are shaded slightly in blue and painted on with a very fine brush.

ANTIQUED PAEONY CUPBOARD

Old original hand-painted pieces of furniture, with their worn, earthy colours are very beautiful but increasingly difficult and expensive to get hold of. A lot are now in museums and it is worth going to see them if you can to pick up ideas for colours and patterns. The techniques described in this book will help you to reproduce the patterns and brush strokes, but, if you wish, you can also imitate the mellowing effect of a hundred years' wear and tear without spending a lot of extra time and effort. A plain old piece of furniture, or even a new one, can be decorated and prematurely 'aged' to fool your friends and provide a lovely piece for your home. Even better, you don't have to worry about your furniture being too delicate or priceless for every day use.

Ours was an old cupboard, painted in white gloss and bought at an auction sale. Attractive panelled doors suggested painting it in the style of Bavarian furniture of the 17th or 18th centuries, so we chose a suitable simple floral design and deep colours – greens, blues and reds – that looked very bright at first but were later toned down by the antiquing process.

DRAGGING

You can often drag paint over an existing painted surface. The faint traces of the original that show through will only add to the antique effect. First key the surface by rubbing it down with coarse sandpaper, making sure that any flaky paint is removed – any bare areas can then be given a touch of acrylic primer. Next, apply a coat of eggshell paint as the base colour (we used green). It will not cover the gloss particularly well in one coat, producing instead the patchy effect that is needed. When painting, drag the brush in the direction of the grain of the wood, then leave it to dry overnight.

The next stage is to paint in the panels that will hold the design. We used a creamy off-white with a hint of grey to give a mellow effect. To draw in the panels on the top of the cupboard, we measured the panels on the doors and reproduced them on the flat top to more or less the same width, using chalk and a ruler. The panels could then be painted in, over the green, using a 5cm (2in) household paintbrush. After painting your panels, leave them to dry overnight.

When dry, key the surface by rubbing it gently with fine sandpaper, especially if you are applying a water-based paint to an oil-based surface. If the paint looks a bit thin, don't worry, as this will add to the aged effect.

PAINTING A PAEONY

The same simple technique is used to paint all the paeonies. Block in the background shape and colour of the flower, then paint a pink dot, placing it where you imagine the centre of the flower would lie if the flower were viewed from the side. About halfway between the first dot and the edge of the flower, and at an angle of 45 degrees to it (to the left if the flower, as in the picture, is going to face right, and vice versa), put in another, smaller dot. These are your points of reference for painting the petal outlines.

Starting from the larger dot, make an elongated tear-shaped stroke, curving down to the smaller dot. Make a second stroke on the other side, to match it. Make two more strokes, again one at each side, rising above the first strokes and curving down to meet them. Then make a fifth stroke above the larger dot.

Fill in the remaining petals, working first down one side then the other: again use elongated tear-shaped strokes, starting from the centre of the topmost stroke of the first grouping and curving down and in towards the centre.

ANTIQUING

You can make your own antiquing mixture, using approximately 2.5cm (1in) of dark oil colour from the tube – here we used Van Dyke brown, but any earth colour, like raw umber, burnt umber or black could be used, or any mixture of these. This is mixed to a paste with two tablespoons of white spirit or turpentine. This quantity will go quite a long way.

If it is too thin, add half a teaspoon of dark brown eggshell paint. To multiply the recipe up, use 5cm (2in) of oil paint, half a cup of white spirit and one teaspoon of eggshell paint. You can also produce a paler antique effect, sometimes called French antique finish, by adding a little white eggshell paint to your mixture.

Paint on the mixture, keeping your strokes in the direction of the grain of the wood.

After a few minutes, and making sure the mixture does not get too dry, take a piece of kitchen paper and begin to wipe it off. The mixture is thin enough to run into every tiny crevice and brush stroke and the kitchen paper is bobbly, both of these facts combining to produce an interesting, dragged effect. Again, wipe along

the grain of the timber. Rub all over, removing as much as you need to leave your darkest tone.

Next, take a clean piece of kitchen paper and gently massage the paint away from the areas that you want to look lightest, for example the centre of the panel. We found that our mixture took off a little of the acrylic paint but this only increased the worn

effect. Leave those areas where dirt would normally collect darkest: crevices at the sides and bottom, for example.

Leave the cupboard to dry a day or two before varnishing. Matt varnish looks the most suitable for an antique effect. After two to three weeks it is often worth buffing up the surface with polish or a tinted wax.

1

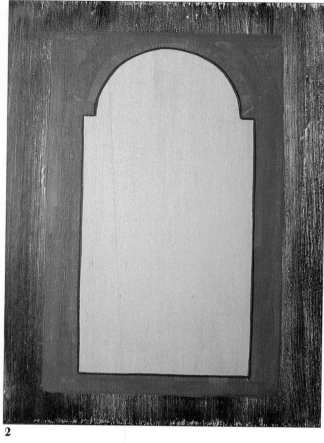

2

STEP 1

After the green and cream base coats had dried, the inner border was drawn, using chalk and a ruler, with a saucer as a guide for the arch at the top of the panel: we measured in by 1.5cm (½in) and drew an inner line along the bottom and the sides, coming in a little and then drawing round the saucer at the top. For the panels at the top of the cupboard, the saucer was used at each end. The old-fashioned coral red was mixed by adding a little red and burnt sienna PVA to apricot silk vinyl. Block in the border, using a pure sable or hog's hair square-ended oil-paint brush – no. 6 or 8 – following the grain of the wood with your brush strokes.

STEP 2

When the paint is dry, paint a fine blue acrylic line between the border and the off-white panel, using a special coachliner brush – no. 1 or 2 – to keep the line straight (see Hearts, Flowers and Lovers).

Using a turquoise blue emulsion paint, paint a wide border all the way round the panels on each door. This border must also be marked out before painting, but this time use a ruler and a series of pencil dots on the green background. We made this border the same width as our ruler to save measuring. Later, further lines will be added, producing the effect of *trompe l'oeil* panelling. Don't worry about perfect brush marks here as the antiquing process will tend to cover any irregularities.

STEP 3

The main panel design is drawn in with chalk. We chose a primitive floral design, a combination of very simple flowers. Chalk lines down the centre of the panel vertically and horizontally divide it into quarters and determine its central point so that the design can be more easily placed. Draw the urn first and then the plants growing out of it, making sure that the leaves are strong enough to achieve a balanced look.

STEP 4

Begin painting by blocking in the main colours. The two bottom flowers and one at the top are blocked in with white, leaving the brush strokes showing and creating a rounded effect for what will later be paeony type blooms. Then block in the pale pink flowers and the bluebell shapes in blue. The leaves are simply defined with single brush strokes of green paint. The large tulip-type flower at the top is painted using a large sable watercolour brush – no. 9 or 12. Take the brush stroke from the bottom of the flower and bring it up, so that it curves outwards and ends in a point for the petals. Remember that the original traditional painting style was not particularly proficient, so if your lines are a bit uneven, don't worry – it only adds to the charm.

3

4

STEP 5

Paint in the details of the paeonies, then go back over the entire painting, accentuating everything by shading and highlighting. Starting at the top with the tulips, fill in the turned-back petals with yellow ochre, then use a darker shade, made by adding a little burnt umber, to shadow them. Use a no. 3 or 4 brush to add the shadows, putting lines down the right-hand sides of the petals and a very thin line down the centre, with small strokes at either side.

All the leaves are shaded with a darker green on the side away from the light, which is imagined to come from the top left-hand corner. For the shadow on the bluebells, use a mixture of blue, green and burnt umber to shade beneath and to the right-hand side of each floret. The other side is highlighted with a lighter shade of blue and white.

For the centre paeony, mix up a very thin wash of pale pink and brush this over that half of each of the petals which would look lighter.

5

6

7

The panel completed, you can now tackle the *trompe l'oeil* panelling effect on the outside border. The border has already been painted the flat colour, as described in step 2. Our pictures show the border without the centre panel filled in so that you can see more of it clearly. Use a combination of dark lines and light lines: every time you put a line on the top and left outside, balance it with one on the right and bottom inside, and vice versa.

8

STEP 8

Using a small coachliner brush and a deeper shade of blue than the border itself, paint two parallel lines along the top and down the left-hand side of the inner edge of the border. Paint two corresponding lines at the bottom and right-hand side, but this time close to the outer edge of the border.

9

STEP 9

Paint two parallel lines in white close to the outer edge of the border along the top and down the left-hand side, then close to the inner edge along the bottom and right-hand side. Paint a slightly thicker, single white line, running alongside the two dark lines along the top and left-hand side and along the bottom and right-hand side.

Mix up a slightly darker blue, using turquoise and green, and paint dark blue lines to correspond with the last set of white lines. Working from the outer edge inwards, the top and left-hand sides now read: two white lines, one dark blue, one white line and two dark blue. The positioning is exactly reversed on the bottom and right-hand sides.

STEP 6

Switching to green paint, touch in the small leaves of the orange flowers and their green centres. Also add the little leaves between the flower at the bottom, using the same tear-shaped brush stroke.

The two bottom big flowers are given a little of the white wash to accentuate the light. The orange hoop-shaped flowers are accentuated with a series of tiny lines going up the petals, using a dark red paint. The leaves are shaded as before. A deeper yellow ochre is used for the urn, to add shading under the rim and in lines down the body where it undulates, and also underneath the right-hand side of its bulbous shape, to make a shadow at that point. To add the highlights, a very diluted white line was painted beside these shadows and to the left-hand side of the centre of the rim. The blue flowers at the bottom of the design are given a puddle of yellow, dotted off a small brush into the centre of each bloom.

OLD-ROSE CHEST OF DRAWERS

Second-hand furniture bargains are perfect for trying your hand at some of our decorative techniques. If the timber is good enough, it can be stripped, stained and varnished before you apply your motif, but even this isn't necessary unless you particularly want the natural-wood look. Where paint is in reasonable condition, it simply needs rubbing down and repainting in the base colour of your choice before you start on the more interesting work. Even large pieces like our chest of drawers can be picked up quite cheaply in their original neglected state, or purloined from friends and neighbours.

Inexpensive but dull new furniture may also benefit from a little extra decoration to add that touch of class and originality. In fact this project piece is new, made from medium density fibreboard (MDF): it is a rather heavy piece of furniture but its pretty shape suggested plenty of design possibilities. Drawers and doors, knobs, finger plates and panels may all give rise to creative ideas, and can be linked, matched or scaled up and down as required.

For our design, we took our inspiration from a piece of floral print fabric featuring a trellis design of ribbons, glorious overblown roses and flowers in coral pink, lime green, and a kind of grey-tinted turquoise on an ivory background. Careful not to be overambitious, we selected only several elements of

the detailed design to translate onto our chest: the main roses and their leaves, which were in two different tones of green.

The chest should first be sealed with white acrylic paint – if you are working on an old piece of furniture, check for repairs and then strip and seal or sand it smooth to key the surface, preparing it for the paint. After this, it should be given two coats of its base colour – we used a grey green – in either silk vinyl or eggshell. Rub down gently after each coat, to maintain a perfectly smooth surface.

We decided to place our floral design within a diamond-shaped panel in imitation of the trellis pattern of the fabric. On the top and side panels the diamond design would be bordered with a ribbon, to match the fabric; because of their narrow shape, the drawer fronts had to be decorated with a more elongated version of the diamond.

When all the decorative painting has been added, as shown in the steps, varnish the chest of drawers, using a matt finish for a softer effect than gloss. To enhance the beautifully-aged appearance you can also antique it (see Antiqued Paeony Cupboard). Some two to three weeks after the last process, wax and buff the chest to produce a subtle patina. Tinted wax, available in a wide range of shades from pine to walnut, will further enhance the aged effect.

SHADING THE LEAVES

The leaves are painted in a mixture of shades: start by blocking in the basic shape of the leaf with a flat coat of paint in one of two colours. One colour was made by mixing green, turquoise and white, and the other by mixing green, white and lemon yellow. These colours are mixed quite thickly and applied with a no. 9 brush.

When the base colour is dry, go over each leaf with a deeper hue of the appropriate colour, indicating the shadows and veining. Use a smaller – no. 4 – brush and imagine the light to come from one corner. (Make sure that this creates the same shadow as on the ribbon and roses.)

Using the same colour, but adding a touch of brown to both to darken them slightly, accentuate some but not all – between a third and a half – of the shadows already put in.

The straightforward diamond shapes were made by drawing in the central horizontal and vertical lines, marking points in from the edges (here, 5cm (2in) in from the sides and 7.5cm (3in) in from the top and bottom) and then joining the points with a chalk and ruler.

STEP 1

First mark the outlines of the design area in chalk. To paint in the background coat of the panels we used a fairly large (no. 7) hog's hair oil painting brush – a flat, squarish or filbert shape is good for block painting. We used a cream colour, available in silk vinyl or eggshell finish – if you match the type of paint to your base coat it will adhere much more easily. It is possible to mix up your own paint using white emulsion or silk vinyl with a little artists' acrylic colour added. This is a useful technique if you can't find the exact colour you want. Put a little of your tube colour into a jam jar or paint kettle, add a spoonful of water, then plenty of white, and stir well.

Fill in within the chalk lines of your panel; you don't have to be absolutely precise because you will be going over it later with your straight border designs.

When blocking in your base coat, use the bulk of the brush to paint the centre part and the tip for the edges. A single coat can look a little patchy but this may be desirable if you are trying to achieve an aged effect. You should always move your brush in the same direction as the grain of the wood if your piece of furniture is timber; or from side to side on drawers and from top to bottom on side panels to create that effect on other materials. If you don't want an antique or aged effect, wait until the first coat is dry, then put on a second, adding a little white if necessary to make the colour a little more opaque.

1

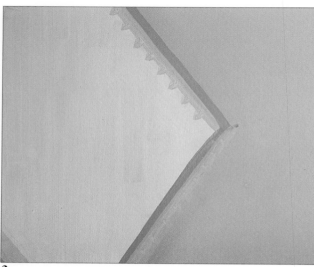

2

3

STEP 2

When the panels have dried, paint the ribbons that surround them. These are painted free-hand, using a coachlining brush with 6.5cm (2½in) long bristles. First rub the area where the line is going to run, using wire wool or sandpaper, to make sure that the paint will adhere. We used acrylic paint, which is fairly translucent, mixed on a plate to the right consistency – thickish and creamy rather than runny.

Imagine the light to come from one side and paint in two lines, one on either side of the chalked line: on the light side of the panel, the outer line is paler and the inner line a darker blue green; on the dark side, this is reversed. Paint all the dark lines first, then mix in a little white and paint the lighter lines. To add to the effect, you can use a slightly thicker brush for the first lines and change to a thinner one for the second set of lines.

Put in bobbles along the edge of the ribbon: load a large round watercolour brush – no. 8 or 9 – with paint and touch the surface where you want a bobble, allowing a blob to slide off. Allow the paint to dry before moving to the next stage.

STEP 3

Next paint in the bows. Start by blocking them in, using the pale colour and working by eye. Wipe any mistakes away with a damp cloth. When the paint is dry, use a darker shade, mixed with grey rather than black for a softer effect, to mark in the diamond and square shapes that give the bows their three-dimensional effect.

STEP 4

When the bows are completely dry, the panel is ready for the main design. This is sketched in chalk to give a rough idea of where the leaves and flowers should lie. The crossed lines are redrawn to mark the centre point.

It is also important at this stage to decide the shape, size and position of knobs or drawer pulls for your piece of furniture. Even if you don't put them on, mark in their position with chalk so that you can be sure they won't obscure the design and make a nonsense of it.

The pattern was drawn, using variable combinations of flowers and leaves to match those on the fabric, but without the panels looking identical. The motifs were adapted to suit the individual size of the panels, with fewer flowers in the smaller ones. Odd numbers seem to look better in groups than even ones, so there are many combinations with groups of three, five and seven. The shapes only need to be roughed in – circles for the roses for example and the outside limit of the leaves. You should aim for a flowing design that fits together neatly rather than filling in any detail at this stage. To paint in the design, we found that the best approach was to paint one complete panel first – preferably one that is most hidden – to check the effect, before working through all the panels systematically, taking one colour or motif type at a time.

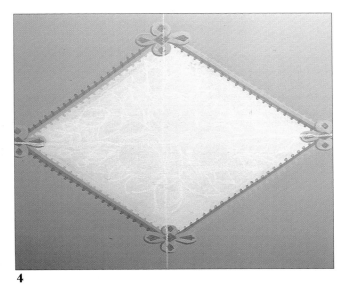

4

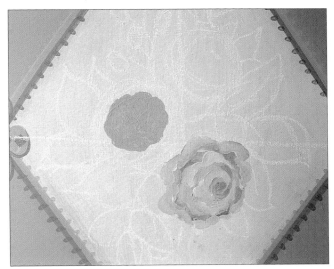

5

6

STEP 5

Paint the roses first, one or two at a time, mixing up a mid-strength colour of coral pink using red, yellow and white paint. Generally the bigger the brush the better – for preference a no. 9 – to block in the simple ball shapes. Use the same technique for the rosebuds, brushing in an oval rather than a circle as for the blooms.

STEP 6

While each rose of this colour is still wet, mix up a deeper shade and select a smaller brush (no. 4) to put in a dot for the centre point and to shade the underside of the orb a little. Next, put in some petals on the opposite side to the place where you imagine the shadows to be. By pressing down on the tip of the brush almost to the ferrule then lifting up to the tip and pressing down again in a continuous motion, you will produce the desired wobbly effect. Using flat colour, also paint in the rose buds (but not their sepals and stems) at this stage.

S T E P   7

Next mix a little white into your original colour to lighten it and add a few more layers of petals on the darker side of the orb, using the same wobbling technique and a no. 9 brush. Leave a little line of deeper pink in the original orb to give the effect of shadow and continue to build up the petals in layers, mixing a further, lighter shade, when this seems necessary. This is sufficient to produce the rough impression of an overblown rose: detail will come later.

7

8

S T E P   8

After the roses have been roughly painted, the leaves are added. Also paint the short stems and sepals of the rose buds. To paint sepals, simply press with your brush at the bottom of the stroke, then raise the brush as you move it upwards, so that only the tip is touching the panel when you reach the top of the sepal. Finally, give the roses a final touch of shading. Deepen their hearts a little and accentuate the darkest creases between the petals. When the main painting is dry use a small – no. 4 – brush and a slightly deeper shade of pink in one or two of the crevices, then a lighter colour (almost white) to highlight the tips of some of the petals.

9

S T E P   9

To finish off, you may like to highlight the leaves too. This can be done with a thin watery white wash, applied down the imagined light side of the leaves. A thin wash of raw or burnt umber can be washed all over if the colour comes out a bit bright and needs toning down a little.

FANTASY FLOWER TABLECLOTH

Decorating your own tablecloth can be as simple or elaborate as you wish: a coloured border to match a set of napkins or china plates; or a magnificent painted floral display of blooms and foliage to create the centrepiece at that special dinner or tea party. Most fabric paints – we used opaque paints for our design – are colourfast once ironed to the manufacturer's specifications, so your cloths will be as practical as those bought from your local store, yet be highly original at a fraction of the cost. As well as cloths for the dining table, you may like to decorate one – or a pair, to cover those small circular chipboard tables popular beside the bed or sofa. Match yours to suit your furnishing scheme, adapting the design from a wallpaper, fabric or bedlinen pattern.

We decided to paint a circular cloth to go down to the floor over a round table. Rather than just painting a border design, we planned an ambitious and exotic pattern of leaves and flowers that could be adapted to suit any colour scheme and any size or shape of cloth.

The individual components can be put together in an infinite variety of ways to create your own designs.

To make your own tablecloth, measure your circular table from edge to floor and double it, then measure the diameter of the table and add this to the existing figure. Add 5cm (2in) for hems, and cut sufficient lengths to make a square when joined (allow for seams). It is neater to use a complete width as the centre panel and trim other widths to an equal measurement to be seamed on at each side. Join the pieces to make a square, then fold the fabric into four and draw a quarter circle: use a pin at the centre point and join it to the marking chalk with a piece of string half the length of the finished cloth plus 2.5cm (1in); mark a quarter circle, then cut through all four layers of fabric. Turn under 6mm (¼in) and then 2cm (¾in) all around the circle and hem.

To protect the finished design, set the paints by ironing the cloth on the reverse side at the appropriate heat setting for the fabric.

SHADED FABRIC PAINTING

The flowers, leaves and even the stalks are all painted in a blend of colours – a technique that is simple but very effective.

For the flowers, start by using fairly dark colour and a stiff hog's hair brush – no. 8 or 10 – and take the paint straight from the pot or tube so that it is not too runny. Paint from the base of the petals, stopping before you reach the outer edge.

While the paint is still

slightly wet, start to mix white with the pink, moving upwards towards the ends of the petals and highlighting the individual petals by leaving a space line between them.

Continue to blend in more white until by the edge of the petals the colour is almost white, accentuating the three-dimensional effect.

The paint tends to blur

a little at the edges, so the design is given a sharper outline with a waterproof fabric pen. Black was used here, but gold or silver would have been equally effective.

STEP 1

This leaf and flower were highlighted in white as already described. The stem was painted in the same way, but using a no. 6 brush.

STEP 2

They were outlined for greater definition, then veins were added to the leaf and black dots to the flower centre, also with the fabric pen.

STEP 3

A different type of flower made up of individual petal segments was given exactly the same blended treatment and outlined in black.

STEP 4

This bell-shaped flower was made up of three irregular ovals elongated into a point. Dark shaded points between the segments gives a three-dimensional effect, while black outlining sharpens up the design.

STEP 5

Buds employ a similar elongated oval shape and white blending. Leaves were coloured half green and half yellow before being outlined.

STEP 6

The central flower of our cloth design is made up from 16 simple coloured and shaded petal shapes, radiating from a central circle. Note how the shaggy outline of the centre and the series of pollen dots executed with the black pen add a realistic touch.

CHAPTER FIVE

DECORATIVE DESIGNS WITH FRUIT

Fruit offers a similar range of decorative possibilities to that of flowers, and has a comparable appeal. The shapes are simple and easy to block in, the simple addition of shadows and highlights in the right place producing a convincing three-dimensional effect.

Colours can be bright to exploit the primary shades of yellow banana, red cherry, green apple and the self-descriptive orange, or faded into soft sugary pastels, less garish earthy shades or even a stylish monochromatic effect in imitation of hand carving or old Delft-ware. Segmented pineapples and split pomegranites are frequently seen as part of the group for their interesting light-and-shade effects. Like flowers, fruit look best closely arranged in groups and linked by simple foliage.

Naturally, a fruit design looks completely at home in the kitchen or dining room, translated onto kitchen cupboards, wooden chair backs or seats, table mats, cloths, napkins and walls. Use fruit motifs to create a continuous border – a grape vine, bramble or wild strawberries are perfect here; or devise centrepieces of fruit spilling out of baskets, bowls or a horn of plenty. Sprigs of cherries or strawberry plants, complete with foliage, make useful incidental designs or can be used as part of a main theme.

ENAMEL-PAINTED COFFEE POT

Tinware is inexpensive and fun, and covers a whole range of items that are equally at home in a country kitchen, on a boat, at a picnic table or gracing the table at an informal family dinner. After a few years' wear and tear, tinware does tend to look a bit tatty; repainting worn or chipped pieces with a bright, new design can give it a new lease of life and a great deal of enjoyment to you. Shapes tend to be quite simple, so you can give your imagination full rein, imitating traditional tole or bargeware designs, or coming up with your own folk-inspired ideas. If you use enamel rather than acrylic paints, your finished items should be sturdy enough for reasonable everyday use.

This old coffee pot seemed to suggest a border design, so the bottom 2.5cm (1in) or so was marked off with masking tape. Because the pot has a small bulge near the bottom as a form of self lining, many small pieces of tape were needed.

Using car enamel paints to produce a dense, very matt effect, the uncovered area was spray-painted with two coats of matt black. To get the best effect when using aerosol paints and to avoid runs, stand well back and apply the paint in a fine spray: several fine coats are always better than one thick one. You will need a screen behind the object to take the excess paint around the edges. Keep the room well ventilated and wear a disposable face mask.

PAINTING WITH ENAMELS

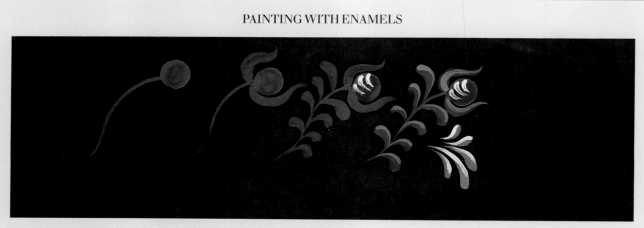

Enamel paints are not really difficult to use, but they are thick and can look rather blobby. It is important to apply them in layers, as shown here for the main design and the border design of the coffee pot, allowing each colour and shade to dry thoroughly overnight before you apply the next.

To make the leaves shown here, for example, you must start by painting the entire leaf shape in mid-green; allow this to dry overnight, and then paint the lighter green highlights on top. When this has had a chance to dry, you can add the final touches of white. This is time-consuming, but if you do not wait until the previous layer has dried, the next one will stick to it and the work will be ruined.

One of the advantages of using these paints is that the layers build up into a pleasantly raised effect, which can be incorporated into the design, giving a rounded feeling to the berries.

STEP 1

When the black paint has dried, the masking tape is removed and the border area is painted with a white lacquer paint, chosen for its extremely glossy, japanned finish. The paint, which is not particularly easy to handle as it is thin and runs easily, should be applied with a short hog's hair painting brush, shaped like a filbert. Again, you will find that two thin coats are better than one thicker one. The paint must be allowed to dry for around six hours between coats.

A matching white border may also be applied to the lid – seen here in its finished state. Drawing straight lines around a circular surface can be tricky so it is a good idea to use a guide. In this case, a small ramekin from the kitchen proved to be the ideal size for the outer edge of the border, while the lid from the can of aerosol paint provided a perfect second line about 1.2cm (½in) in towards the centre of the lid. The lines can be drawn with a pencil. You will find narrow borders relatively easy to paint if you use a short hog's hair oil-painting brush and hold it horizontally to get a reasonably level line.

The base colours must be left to dry for 24 hours before the details are added in modelmakers' enamels. These are available in small pots and produce a high gloss, very hard-wearing finish.

STEP 2

Draw the design initially in blackboard chalk, which produces a clear outline sufficient for such a simple style and which can be rubbed off easily. Simple leaves and berries were chosen here, in imitation

1

2

3

of tole-painting or the boatmen's Van Dyking, and strong red and green paints were selected to reinforce that effect. Paint simple branches and leaves first, then add extra leaves in a paler green to create a light and shadow effect. The same green is also used to highlight the existing leaves. Using the same simple one-stroke technique, the spout and handle are decorated with green leaves, highlighted in the paler green.

The design must be allowed to dry before highlights of plain white can be added to the red balls and the paler green leaves. On the white borders, a bright green and red pattern is applied. This was planned to match the main design and suggests simple leaves and flowers, indicated by dots and single strokes of the brush. As with any border that is circular, this design has to be carefully plotted in to make sure it fits neatly. Marking the horizontal centre of the border, a thin green line is painted as described above.

STEP 3

In the centre between each division, a big stroke is flanked by two little ones on either side of it; the same technique is employed on the bottom side of the line too. The red dots are put in by eye and when dry, highlighted with a dot of white paint.

When the paint has completely dried, the coffee pot is given two coats of eggshell poly-urethane varnish for real durability and long use.

EXOTIC FRUITS KITCHEN PANEL

A run of plain kitchen units is often dull, while a hand-decorated kitchen is prohibitively expensive – if you call in a professional. Yet, painting a simple design on the doors of their own units is well within the capacity of most people. The investment of a little time and effort can transform a budget installation into a kitchen with star quality. If you follow the recommended technique you will achieve a uniformity of pattern, but the slight variations between images are all part of the charm of this type of painting, so do not worry if each door in a completed run is not identical to the others.

The units featured here were made of MDF (medium density fibreboard), a good, sturdy and inexpensive alternative to timber. This takes paint very well, producing a lovely smooth finish, slightly akin to that on a plastered surface. You can, however, achieve equally successful results on wood or plywood.

We were aiming at an 18th-century, monochromatic look, rather like carved wood, so we kept to a very limited number of colours. In this case, an eggshell paint was used for the pale yellow background, and the design was painted in acrylic paints, using varying dilutions of Venetian red, sometimes mixed with raw sienna to lighten the effect.

Acrylic paints, as long as they are not mixed with white, have a certain translucency, and the idea was to use this to highlight the painting from beneath, allowing traces of the pale yellow background to show through the overpainting. This type of monochromatic painting is a good way for a beginner to experiment and achieve a three-dimensional effect without the design looking too garish or busy. The colours could, of course, be chosen to suit the décor of your own kitchen.

Before you start to prepare the doors for painting and transfer the pattern given on pages 140-41, first roughly sketch the outline in chalk. You may find that the shape of your unit doors dictates minor adjustments to the pattern – perhaps it needs to be elongated or made wider (the size and shape of the bunch of grapes can easily be changed and other fruits added or taken away, as necessary). When you are happy with the pattern, the next stage is to prepare the units for painting. The door shown here was stripped and given a coat of primer, followed by an undercoat. After this it was given two coats of eggshell paint in pale yellow. Once the base paint has been applied, it is essential to key the surface to receive the acrylic paint. This is done by rubbing it down with fine sandpaper or flourpaper.

RIBBON PAINTING

It is important that the ribbon should look natural and flowing, and this is much easier to achieve if you work freehand. This is simpler than it looks, though it would be a good idea to practise on a spare piece of card first if you have never used the technique before. There is no need even to draw the outline in chalk. If you want a guideline, draw in a rough chalk line and add the detail when you paint. Use a no. 4 or 6 brush and start with the tip loaded with Venetian red. Draw it a short way, curving it upwards and then, as you turn the bend, push down on the brush to widen the line. Keeping the flow continuous, lift the brush slightly again and paint on with the tip. Continue this way, pressing down and raising the brush in a bouncing motion, zigzagging to create the twisted ribbon effect. Allow the brush to do the work, aiming for a relaxed, fluid effect.

The ribbon may look very realistic and natural as it is, but if you wish to increase the twisted effect by giving the ribbon some shading, take a fine brush and paint in small lines, running across the width of the ribbon, as shown. Imagine where the shadows would lie and where the curve of the ribbon would catch the light, and shade it accordingly.

Go over part of the loop with the darker shade of Venetian red, to indicate what would be the back of the ribbon or tape holding the bunch.

S T E P 1

Put two puddles of paint – Venetian red and raw sienna – on a plate. Use a big brush, no. 8 or 9, and take up a large amount of paint so that it slides off easily. On areas where the paint is less thickly laid on, the underlying surface should show through, like highlights.

Using Venetian red, start by painting the loop and the rounded fruit shapes, painting them roughly at first, as seen in the fruit at the bottom right corner. For the more pointed shapes, such as the pomegranite (leave the centre of this blank at this stage), mix a little raw sienna with the Venetian red, to lighten the tone.

S T E P 2

While the paint is still wet, move the brush in a circular motion over the darker, rounder pieces of fruit to suggest the shape. Imagine where the bottom of the fruit lies and circle round from this point. For the more pointed fruits, work the brush downwards to emphasize the shape. Define the pineapple by drawing the brush in slightly curving diagonal lines, removing a little of the paint, so that the undercolour shows through. Use the tip of the brush to create the trellis effect.

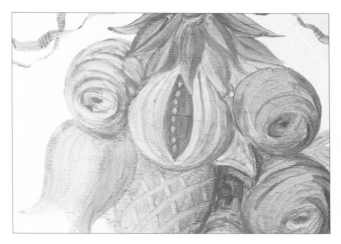

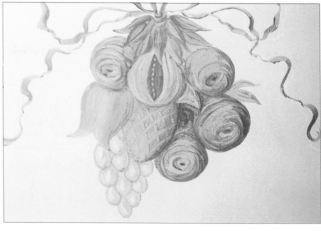

S T E P 3

Fill in the centre of the pomegranite with a thin, watered down layer of Venetian red, then paint in the ribbon. When the main area is dry, use a thicker mixture of Venetian red to go over the centre of the pomegranite again, this time painting around the outlines of the seeds and then filling in the background around them. Using a deep colour wash, go back over the other fruits and the leaves and put in shading, imagining the light to come from one side. At the bottom of each rounded fruit there would be a slight depression, so indicate this by painting in a small shadow, in the shape of a C, on the shaded side of each round fruit.

S T E P 4

Next paint the grapes: using a medium-thick mixture of Venetian red and raw sienna, paint the outlines first and then fill in the centres, using a very diluted, pale wash and painting this on while the outlines are still wet. Blur the wash slightly into the outlines, to soften them, but leave an unpainted highlight.

When the paint has dried it may be necessary to go over the shaded areas a second time, as the acrylic paint is very translucent.

STRAWBERRY CIRCLE

Although there is a wide range of tablemats to be found in the shops, it is often difficult to find exactly what is needed to team up with your china or to match your décor. Fortunately, it is quite simple to design and make your own, picking out a theme from your tablelinen, perhaps, or even a motif from your dining room curtains. This also enables you to choose the perfect colours rather than make do with something that is almost, but not absolutely, right.

We made our mats from 6mm (¼in) plywood discs about 23cm (9in) in diameter, which were produced quite cheaply by our local carpenter/joiner. Although our mats are circular, it would be just as easy to produce a square, rectangular, or even a hexagonal design.

Before you start to sketch in the design, first prepare the mats. To produce as smooth a surface as possible, rub over the mats with a proprietary wall filler, mixed to a fairly thick paste, then scrape across the grain of the wood to remove any excess. When this has dried, rub the mats down with fine sandpaper.

Next, prime the mats with wood primer, then give them a coat of undercoat followed by two coats of your chosen base colour, using either a silk vinyl or eggshell finish (eggshell produces better definition between the colours and a crisper finish). When you have applied the final coat, rub over the surface with wire wool or flourpaper to create a fine surface for the design.

When you have painted in the design, as described, you will want to protect it. There may be a centre within reach that offers a polyurethane sealing service; if so, this is an excellent way to keep your mats in top condition. If not, you will have to apply a couple of coats of matt or gloss polyurethane varnish to offer some protection from heat and water. Remember, however, that each coat has a yellowing effect and that gloss generally offers better protection than matt. A final touch is to cut circles of green baize or felt to size and glue one to the reverse side of each mat, to give it a professional finish and prevent it from scratching your table.

SERRATED-EDGED LEAVES

Leaves are a favourite freehand painting motif and they can be easily and effectively created without using a second colour. Paint your leaves and while the colour is still wet, draw the tip of your brush down the centre of the leaf and in ribbed lines to the outside of its outline. If you draw the paint brush just beyond this outline, you will produce the appearance of a serrated edge as on rose or strawberry leaves. Using the brush in this way removes a tiny amount of paint and produces a three-dimensional and shadowed effect, without the need for a second colour. It is important to work while the paint is still wet.

S T E P 1

Using a pair of compasses and a pencil, draw the inner and outer circles of the border. You will need to find the centre point of the mat to position the compass point. The easiest way to do this is to draw a square on paper, each side the diameter of the mat – in this case 23cm (9in). Draw in the diagonals from corner to corner and make sure that the square has been drawn accurately by checking that the diagonals cross at right angles. Place each mat on the square and, using chalk, draw in the diagonals across the mat to find the centre point. When you have found the centre, draw in the outer circle of the border, 3mm (1/8in) in from the edge, and the inner circle 5.3cm (2 1/8in) in from the edge.

S T E P 2

Using the segmented template, mark the ten, evenly spaced, segment divisions at the outer edge of the mat. Using a ruler and chalk, laying the ruler across the centre point of the mat and each segment division in turn, make chalk lines dividing the border into ten equal segments. Use a protractor to check that the segments radiate evenly at 36 degree angles from the centre of the mat, and make corrections if necessary. Next, chalk in small arcs across the ends of the segment dividers, touching the outer and inner circles alternately, as shown. Link these to form a continuous line curving between the inner and outer borders – as you are using chalk you can wipe away any unsatisfactory curves and start again. Also continue the arcs round in curls to form what will be the stalks of the strawberries .

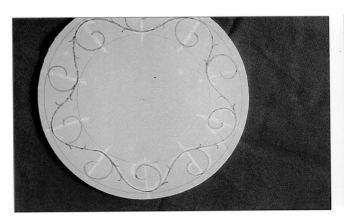

S T E P 3

When these basic lines have been drawn in, you can start painting. Acrylic paints are used for the design and any mistakes can easily be wiped off with a damp cloth before the paint has dried. Using a fine brush (no. 1 or 2) and green paint, paint along the wavy line and the curly lines of the stalks. Allow these lines to dry before you move to the next stage.

S T E P 4

The leaves can be painted in freehand but you could sketch them first in chalk or with a very faint pencil line. As long as they fill the space pleasantly, total uniformity is not important. The leaves are arranged in groups of three, with four slightly different groupings according to the shapes of the spaces left between the curls. Use a no. 4 brush and load it with green paint, filling in as much of the space as possible by blocking the leaves in flatly with the brush. While the paint is still wet, draw the tip of the brush down the stem and across to create the veining. These lines can be accentuated later with a darker shade of green, but this is time-consuming and not really necessary.

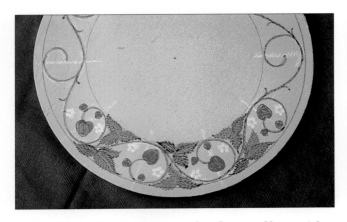

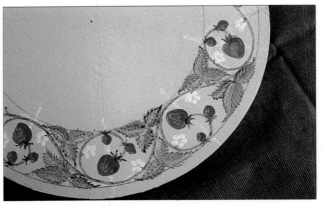

S T E P 5

The next stage is to fill in the strawberry outlines. Block in the shapes with flat red paint. There is no need to draw each strawberry first – just paint a shape like a simple heart, but with the points more rounded.

When this has dried, use green paint and a fine brush – no. 1 or 2 – to paint the hull.

Finish by shading in one side of each strawberry, using a watery mixture of red and green. If you wish, make a runny mixture of white and yellow and, again with a fine brush, add dots to the strawberries to make the pips. Paint all the big strawberries first and then the smaller ones, fitting them roughly into the spaces that remain. For the small white flowers, use a fairly large – no. 6 or 8 – brush, loaded from a thick puddle of paint. Use this to make five dots to create the five petals of each flower.

S T E P 6

When the flowers and strawberries have dried, go back over the design, using the green paint and a fine brush, and paint in the little stalks and the hulls of the strawberries. Highlight the leaves by making a watery mix of white paint and using this to wash one of each leaf, producing a three-dimensional effect. For consistency, take care to highlight each identical group on the same side, all the way around.

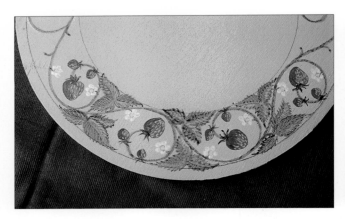

S . T E P 7

Next shade in one side of each strawberry and add pips, as described in Step 5. Delineate the centre of each strawberry flower with a tiny ring of green, then fill the centre with a mixture of white and yellow, to show this up.

S T E P 8

Finish by putting in the red circles that run around the border and highlight its shape. It is not easy to draw an accurate circle. You may be able to use your original pencil lines; if not, you will achieve the best result if you use a special paint brush, such as a shortened coachliner or a fitch (see pages 106-7). These have a very long narrow head, which gives you greater control. Alternatively, if you have a rotating icing turntable, experiment with this, fixing the mat firmly to the centre and then giving the table a spin and lowering your brush onto the mat.

FRUIT BASKET TILE DESIGN

Using ceramic paints, you can design and paint your own highly original tiles. Hand-painted tiles are usually very expensive in the shops but white tiles are cheap and provide the perfect background for your own decorative attempts. You are obviously not going to have the time and facilities to paint hundreds of tiles, but a few can be quickly and easily decorated to create a picture panel or several single picture tiles can be added in a random design to a larger area of bought plain tiles. Small areas of tiles can be used to make a splashback behind a bath or basin, a table top dropped into a wooden frame or a pot stand.

In our example we used a set of nine tiles to make a complete picture – an attractive fruit-inspired tile panel that would look good at the back of the hob or work top. The best effects are those inspired by traditional hand-painted tiles: distinctive blue Delft or strong Spanish geometrics in their Moorish colours. We choose a Delft effect, which uses the minimum of colours to great advantage, providing good practice for shading, highlighting and graduating tones effectively.

The paint used is water based and is recommended for ceramics. The only drawback to this type of paint is that it must be fired if it is to be durable (a domestic oven is suitable for the firing process). Because of this, the tiles must be decorated before they are put in place, and in any case the painting should take place on a flat surface so that the light, watery washes do not run.

USING CERAMIC PAINTS

These water based paints can be used to build up layers of shading, just like watercolours. We did not have greyish Delft blue, so we mixed it from other blues, using a little black to deaden the colour.

Paint the outline, then fill in the features with a very pale, watery wash. Put plenty of this on your brush – if it is too thinly spread there will be brush marks. For the larger areas, use a big brush, such as a no. 8 or 9, filled with paint. Work from the lighter side of each fruit downwards, leaving an unpainted highlight area where you imagine the light to fall.

A slightly wavery line will look more effective when it dries. The blue can be then darkened and the brush loaded with paint to produce rich ovals, with indeterminate, wobbly edges, to suggest plums, again leaving highlights. To fill the triangular gaps between the grapes, other fruits, and the basket – areas that would normally be in shadow – use a smallish brush (no. 3 or 4) and with a thick mix of dark blue paint. The same dark paint and a smaller brush (no. 1 or 2) was used for the dark line around the centre of the daisies and the lines of shading on the petals, the tiny stalks and leaves on the apples, and the basket trim.

S T E P   1

Lay the tiles edge-to-edge
on a flat surface and draw
the design outlines on
them, using a soft pencil –
a 2B or 4B is easier to use
than an HB pencil. It is
easier to make sure that
you achieve a balanced
effect if you draw the
design from the bottom
upwards, starting with the
basket. Make a pencil dot
where you imagine the
stalk of each fruit to lie.

Next, make a fairly thick
puddle of paint on a saucer
and, using a small – no. 1
or 2 – sable watercolour
brush, paint over the
pencil lines, then leave the
paint to dry.

S T E P   2

Use a very thin wash and a
large brush to start filling
in the larger fruits,
imagining the light to
come from one specific
source, and therefore
creating an impression of
light and shade. Use the
wash in the same way over
the centre of each daisy
and for the paler fruits,
such as the grapes on the
light side of the bunch.
Leave a little white
highlight on each grape
and a shadow where each
overlaps the top of the one
below; this gives a feeling
of roundness.

Paint down the basket
struts, using a single brush
stroke for each strut, for a
light from one side would
throw the undulations of
the basket into shadow.
Don't worry if there is a
small puddle of paint at the
bottom of each strut as this
will look very effective
when it dries.

Try to keep within the
outlines, but don't try to
wipe any error off with a
damp cloth. Leave it to dry
and correct it later with the
right colour.

S T E P   3

With a slightly deeper,
thicker shade of the blue,
we went over the darker
fruits in the same way as
the first wash, again
imagining that the light
was coming from the top
left-hand corner and
leaving areas of white as
highlights. This slightly
deeper wash was also used
to touch in the edging at
the top and bottom of the
basket.

S T E P   4

The darker wash was then
used to fill in the leaves,
leaving a blank white strip
down the middle of each
leaf and where the veins
would lie either side. This
accentuates their three-
dimensional effect and is
more interesting than just
putting in shadows. The
wash colour was then
darkened just a little more
and used to paint the left-
hand, dark grapes leaving
highlights as we did for the
paler ones.

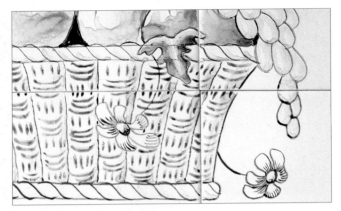

STEP 5

When the shadows already applied to the basket struts were dry, a middle tone – not too dark – was mixed. This was applied with a no. 4 brush in short lines, to give the effect of the horizontal weave of the basket. The technique is similar to that used for the petals: a quick, single flick of the brush. If you do it quickly it won't disturb the paint you have already applied.

STEP 6

Also using a small brush (no. 3 or 4), paint the diamond shaped diagonal lines on the pineapple. This looks rather like a trellis but the lines are slightly curved. Each diamond section is accentuated with a small crescent shape, like an arrow pointing right, to produce a three-dimensional effect.

The vine tendrils are the last stage of the main design and are painted with a no. 2 brush and a puddle of fairly dark paint – take care it is not too runny. The brush should be twisted twice in one direction, then used to describe an S-shaped loop before it is twisted twice in the other direction ending with an S-shaped loop at the bottom.

STEP 7

When the design is complete, paint the border. With a small brush and the deepest colour, draw a simple daisy at each outer corner, with a double line for the centre semi-circle and another for the outside loops. When this has dried, use a slightly bigger brush (no. 3 or 4) and a paler mix, and wash colour between the lines. Next, draw lines between the daisies, using a no. 4 brush and the middle tone of paint. As you lower the tip of the brush to about 6mm (¼in) from each flower you can use your finger to run down the side of the tile pressing the brush gently. Don't start with the tip too near the edge as the brush will spread out slightly 6 to 8mm (¼ to ⅓in). When you remove your brush at the edge you will be left with a little puddle of colour: don't worry – this only adds to its charm.

STEP 8

If you wish to accentuate the border, another row of tiles can be added all round with the lining and half daisy motif applied to the adjoining edge in the same way. You will find they fit neatly together.

When the paint is dry, tiles can be baked in the oven according to manufacturers' recommendations. In this case the oven was pre-heated to 200°C for 15 minutes then lowered to 150°C and the tiles baked for half an hour.

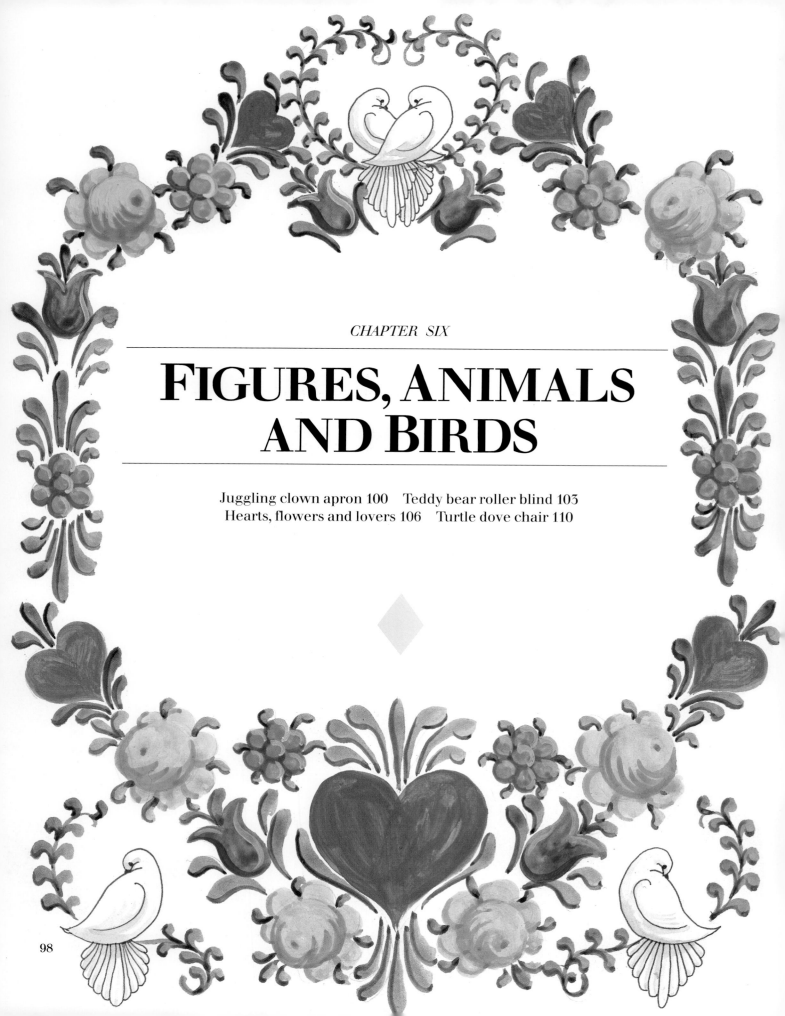

FIGURES, ANIMALS AND BIRDS

If you have a talent for it, figures and animals can be painted realistically, but simple stylized figures, of the type seen on oriental rugs or Egyptian wall paintings, are easy to draw and can be equally effective. Alternatively, you might try your hand at cartoon-type figures, gleaned from comics or picture books. Popular figures in folk art include mythological subjects such as mermaids, gryphons, unicorns and dragons – all of which can be used for a medieval effect – and the perennially popular image of Adam and Eve standing under the apple tree, frequently seen on painted or embroidered marriage gifts.

Down the ages animals have been even more popular as subjects than people, and range from the lion rampant and the other beasts of heraldry, to mystical hares, often depicted in threes with their ears linked in a circular design, or to the horses' heads favoured by Romany artists. Birds, again often with some kind of allegorical meaning, have also put in their fair share of appearances. The dove is a familiar symbol of peace, but also signifies the Holy Spirit or, in pairs, lovers.

Traditional figures look marvellous on borders or used as the centrepiece of a panel. The modern cartoon motifs, on the other hand, are ideally suited to children's clothes, furniture and furnishings, or on the walls of a playroom, and it is generally easy to adapt a child's favourite figure to a usable image.

99

JUGGLING CLOWN APRON

Children's clothes are great fun to decorate because they are small, easy to handle and you can really let your imagination run riot with colours and motifs based on their favourite cartoon characters. This easy apron was cut from an adult pinafore in plain white cotton (a good fabric to use as it can be ironed at a high temperature): it was hemmed all around and tapes were then stitched at the made up neck and sides and the apron was thoroughly ironed so that the fabric would lie completely flat and uncreased. Fabric paints were used straight from the pot for good, flat, solid colour.

When you have finished painting the design and drawing the black outlines, leave it for about two hours before sealing the paint with an iron, according to the manufacturer's instructions.

OUTLINING

In this naive design, ideally suited to a child, unshaded colours are used throughout. To complete the bold, cartoon-like effect, strong outlines are needed to contain the areas of colour and add details. These cover all the original pencil lines and are added in black, using a waterproof fabric pen. Wait until the painted areas have dried, then use the pen to go over all the outlines and all the lines where two colours meet. The pen is also used to draw the details of the eyes, the mouth, and the tufty hair. Be careful when outlining to keep the pen moving at an even pace: if you rest it for a while in one position the ink will soak into the fabric at that point and make a thicker line.

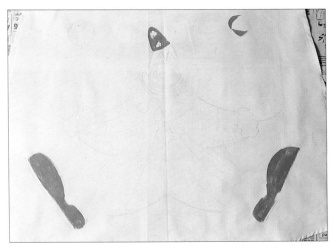

S T E P   1

Before you start painting, iron the apron to remove the creases so that it will lie flat. Arrange it on a firm level surface, securing the sides with weights or heavy books if necessary. Paint tends to pass through thin cotton, so place a thick layer of newspaper below to protect your surface. The easiest and cleanest way to paint is to use one colour at a time and work right through the design. This ensures that you achieve a good balance of colour and also means that you don't have to keep washing your brushes. Use a no. 6 hog's hair oil paint brush with a filbert or square end for the smaller details, and a no. 7 for the larger areas. You cannot use a sable brush as you will not have enough control over it.

S T E P   2

When you have painted the green details, move to the yellow, then paint the nose. Leave a crescent-shaped highlight unpainted – this is the only real piece of highlighting in the entire design.

S T E P   3

When you have painted the nose, add a little yellow to the red, to make it more orangey in colour and distinguish the lips from the nose. The colours do not run into each other, so you do not have to wait until the yellow stripes on the clown's costume have dried before you start painting the red stripes that lie next to them.

S T E P   4

When the remaining colours have been painted, leave the apron to dry for about half an hour before completing the design by drawing in the black outlines and details, as described.

TEDDY BEAR ROLLER BLIND

As with so many of the projects in this book, a hand-painted decoration is used here to transform an inexpensive, plain item into something a little special. Fabric painting is great fun, and a plain roller blind, whether it is white, cream, a pastel or a primary shade, makes a wonderful blank canvas on which you can paint a coordinated border design, a floral panel, a *trompe l'oeil* effect or, as here, a little scene that would delight a small child.

The big teddy and the three smaller ones are based on the same pattern, with only the scale and the position changed, showing how adaptable a single motif can be. If you want to make your own design, you could trace a motif from an old story book, or make a design to match the playroom wallpaper – the possibilities are endless.

We used a plain white blind with a waxed finish that made it less absorbent than an unwaxed fabric and so produced a sharper, brighter image. The teddies were blown up to the correct sizes: we used a photocopying machine with a reducing and enlarging facility. The teddies were then traced in position. The balloons were drawn in freehand, using a soft pencil (the pencil marks would be covered when all the outlines were gone over with a permanent marker). They were positioned at various heights and angles, then the bumble bees were added, filling the remaining large gaps.

DRAWING THE FUR

To give each bear a hazy, fluffy edge, take a permanent black pen or marker (with not too fine a nib) and go all round the outline of each bear with a flicking motion, to give the impression of fur – make small strokes as you might when painting blades of grass. The black pen is also used to draw in the bears' eyes.

1

2

3

4

STEP 1

The design is coloured in with PVA paints. These can be used straight from the tube for extra depth and colour: squeeze the paint directly onto the surface of the blind and then work it in with the brush. You could use special fabric paints, but if the blind will not be washed, PVA is equally suitable and has the advantage that it can be mixed with acrylic or emulsion paints (but not oils) for shaded effects.

Begin by painting the teddies in blocks of yellow. A large, stiff, hog's hair brush, suitable for oil paints, is best for this and can be used to work the paint well into the fabric. Also block in the plain colours for the balloons and the bow ties, again using plenty of colour and the big brush to achieve solid shapes that are dense and even.

STEP 2

While the paint is still wet on the teddies, mix up a brown shade and shade the edges of each teddy with the hog's hair brush, using a kind of dry brush technique. This involves putting the minimum of paint onto your brush (wipe off any visible excess) and scrubbing or blending it round the edges and on the pads and inside of the ears, thereby creating a three-dimensional effect.

STEP 3

When this is dry, add a highlight down the right-hand side of each balloon that is wholly visible (some are partly hidden, so the highlight would not show). Use a single stroke of white paint for each highlight, making it with the tear stroke in which the brush is pressed down firmly to begin with and is then raised until only the tip remains in contact with the surface. While you are using the white paint, take the opportunity to add the white spots to the teddies' bow ties.

The bees are painted next: they look a little fuzzy to begin with, as the fabric blurs the colours a little, but once they have been outlined in black, you will find that they are suitably accentuated. Allow the paint to dry, then take up your permanent black pen or marker and go around each outline, as for the bears. Also draw a circle round each of the balloons and mark in a neck and a string for each.

STEP 4

Quickly executed, this blind does not need a protective varnish, though if you have made it yourself you may wish to give it a coating of roller blind stiffener before hanging it in position.

HEARTS, FLOWERS AND LOVERS

Small accessories around the home make good subjects for your decorative attempts. It can be particularly difficult to find suitable attractive waste paper baskets, but this one is simply cut out of plywood, using a template based on a square shape. The pattern could be designed and dragged to match your living room, bedroom or study, and the receptacle featured here could equally well be used as a planter.

Our designs are based on the popular Pennsylvanian Dutch folk-style figures. These are simply made of component parts so that even an unskilled painter can execute them easily. The scene shown in the photographs depicts a lady, but this can be alternated on the remaining sides of the basket with a painting in the same naive style, in this case showing a kneeling man holding a bunch of flowers.

Waste paper baskets tend to receive hard wear, so it would be wise to finish with two coats of varnish – we used gloss, for a smart, shiny effect. If you want to add a finishing touch, the inside of the basket could also be painted, perhaps in red to match the hearts.

USING A COACHLINER

To paint a reasonably straight line you need a special brush called a coachliner or fitch. This has extremely long bristles ending in a fine point and its length is designed to absorb any small wobbles before they reach the tip.

Start by making a puddle of paint large enough for the whole length of the lining brush. The paint should be fairly runny so that the brush will have a fluid movement and the paint will not dry before you reach the end of the line.

Dip the lining brush into a jar of water (or white spirit if you are using oil-based paints) to moisten it, then stroke it through the puddle of paint until the whole length is covered. You may have to twirl the handle slightly to ensure that the bristles are covered on all sides. When you lift the brush, the weight of the paint will make it droop a little; touch the edge of the plate with the tip of the brush to remove drips.

It is easier to draw the line firmly and steadily if you start as far away as possible and draw the brush towards your body, using your legs and knees to move your body rather than simply moving your elbow and wrist: this will help to prevent your arm shaking.

If you position your feet in the right place to enable you to pull towards the very end of the line you should find that this technique works satisfactorily.

When you start using the brush, place the tip at the beginning of the line and begin to move it slowly towards you, keeping about a half to two-thirds of the brush down. Keep moving slowly along the line with your eyes a little in front

of the tip of the brush – just under the ferrule. Holding your breath will sometimes help you to keep your hand steady. Alternatively, rest your little finger or the side of your hand against the edge of the object that you are decorating.

When you get towards the end of the line, you should start to lift the brush a little. If it proves too difficult to finish the line and lift off the brush without wobbling a little, go over the end a second time, lift the brush and carefully wipe away the excess, using a damp cloth. Keep a damp cloth by your side for any little aberrations. If the line is completely hopeless and the paint has dried, rub it off with wire wool and start again.

S T E P   1

Prime the basket with a coat of acrylic primer followed by a layer of undercoat, rubbing it down after each coat to maintain a smooth surface. Next, give it a coat of eggshell in your chosen base colour (we used turquoise), then rub the surface down once more, using very fine sandpaper or flourpaper to key the surface and ensure that the painted design will adhere to it. The white lines that delineate the edges are painted freehand using a fairly large coachliner brush – no. 4 or 5. You may find it helpful to rest your little finger along the edge of the basket to keep your hand steady. Keep a damp cloth beside you to remove any mistakes.

When the paint has dried, draw a chalk line down the centre of each of the four sides of the waste paper basket and draw horizontal registration lines. Again with chalk, draw a figure on each side: the shapes are all very simple and the figures can easily be drawn freehand. For the lady, start with the jacket, which is essentially just a simple curve; the arm is drawn next – a tear stroke with a ball at the end for the hand; the head is an oval, and the hat and flowers need only be roughly sketched. The kneeling man is equally simple.

1

2

3

S T E P   2

When a design has been drawn on each side, begin to paint the colours, using a fairly large brush – no. 8 or 9 – and acrylic paints mixed with water on a plate. For the lady, we started with the jacket, which was blocked in with blue. If you are painting the man, also start with the jacket.

S T E P   3

Next fill in the skirt. Use yellow ochre, adding a little white to make the paint more opaque. Paint the skirt with downward brush strokes, to give the impression of folds. Rinse the brush and change to a no. 4, then paint the oval outline of the face: a mixture of cadmium red light, a tiny bit of ochre and plenty of white will produce a suitable skin tone and the same colour can be used for the hands. If you are painting the man, you should paint his trousers, and then use the flesh colour for the face and hands. His legs are painted freehand; this is not difficult, but you might like to practise first on a spare piece of card.

STEP 4

When the lady's painted jacket has dried, use plain white to add the frills and apron. Add a little extra water when painting the apron so that the blue shows through and gives a gauzy, muslin impression. A dark blue-grey colour is used for the hair, hat and shadows, giving a softer feel than black. Paint the hat first, then the details of the face: about halfway down the oval, put two dots for the eyes, making sure that they are not too close together, which tends to give a mean look. There is no nose, and the mouth is a very small heart in cadmium red light. Add a little more cadmium light to the existing flesh colour to make the cheeks – just two small circles under the eyes.

Paint the ringlets of hair, then outline the jacket to accentuate it, using the original turquoise colour with a little of the dark grey.

STEP 5

To paint the ribbon on the hat, wait until the hat has dried then use a no. 4 brush loaded with yellow and ochre plus white. To paint the ribbon, start with the tip of the brush under the chin and press the brush down a little as you make the bow, to flatten the shape. Raise the brush a little as you reach the apex of the bow on each side. Make the streamers in the same way, to achieve the thick-and-narrow effect of twisted ribbon.

STEP 6

Finish the detailing of the skirt: ouline it in the original yellow colour with a little of the grey mixed in;

4

5

6

the loops around the lower edge are painted in pure yellow ochre and then, when dry, are outlined with grey mixed into the yellow ochre (use a no. 4 brush for this).

Complete the scene by putting in the border details. Our border, shown here with one side just begun and the other completed, was mainly painted freehand, but we marked in a line at each corner, dividing it in half, so that we knew where the centre of each heart should lie. Draw the hearts in chalk and then work out from these points, drawing bluebells at each side and leaving enough space for the small green leaves. Draw circles to act as guidelines containing the little blue flowers.

The hearts at the corners, on the pinafore and in the bunch of flowers are blocked in with cadmium red light. Don't worry if the corner hearts are not identical – irregularity is part of the charm of this type of painting. The bluebells are painted in turquoise and then, using a slightly lighter blue, the pale blue flowers are painted by making a dot in the centre of the circle and then surrounding it with six more dots.

Next, paint the leaves, sizing them to fit the spaces. Odd numbers look better balanced than even ones, so arrange them in groups of three and five, painting them with simple strokes of the brush. The stalks of the flowers held by the figure are also painted in green.

Finish by highlighting the small blue flowers, using plain turquoise for the shadows and a mixture of turquoise and white for the highlights.

TURTLE DOVE CHAIR

Chairs are perhaps among the cheapest and most accessible of the large items on which you can try out your creative ideas. Although they look fiddly, the back, seat and legs all offer unlimited design possibilities, and the total surface area is never large, so your decoration is quickly finished. Children's chairs like this one are particularly good subjects and can be decorated with a scene from a favourite fairy tale, a cartoon figure or, as in this case, they can be given the traditional charm of folk-style painting and an antiqued finish.

You can antique your chair before or after the design has been painted, then finish with a coat of matt varnish. If you know that the chair will receive considerable wear and tear, and you wish to maintain an antiqued finish, it is best to choose eggshell.

POINTED LEAVES

This leaf technique employs a similar brush stroke to the tear stroke leaves of the design on page 42, but in this case you should use a smaller brush and work in the opposite direction.

First paint the stalk, using a no. 4 brush and then, with the same brush, start from the stem end and describe a kind of flattened 'S' shape. This is made by adjusting the pressure on the brush: first pressing down, then lifting it up. This finishes one half of the leaf.

Bring the brush back to the starting point and paint in the other side of the leaf, using exactly the same technique and again ending at the point of the leaf. You should overlap the two brush strokes slightly to meet at the tip and complete your leaf shape.

STEP 1

The chair shown here was given an undercoat of white, followed by an antique-looking off-white base coat in eggshell. If your chair has already been painted, simply rub it down and make sure that there are no loose particles of paint before you paint the base coat over the existing surface. When the base coat has dried, rub it down with sandpaper to key the surface, then draw the design on the chair seat, using chalk. Draw centre guidelines from top to bottom and from side to side, quartering the seat, then draw the border, chalking in only the wavy lines, at this stage without the leaves. Position the doves one on either side of the centre line, perching them on just a couple of curves curling up into a heart shape behind them.

STEP 2

Next, block in the doves, using fairly thick paint and a no. 8 or 9 watercolour sable or sable-mixture brush. The brush strokes can be fairly random at first, but when the birds have been blocked in, go back over them with the tip of the brush to indicate the main feathers and the cheek bones. The tail feathers are put in with tear strokes, starting at the tip of the tail and working up towards the body.

STEP 3

While the doves are drying, paint the wavy green line and block in the deep pink flowers at the end of each stem. Each flower is painted with just two strokes of the brush – the strokes should start narrow, widen, then narrow at the centre, widen again, and finally narrow to a point, making something like an hour glass shape.

STEP 4

Using the green paint, add the leaves, putting large ones around the border, especially at the points where the smaller branches join the main stem. The smaller leaves can then be painted in, after which you can go back over the flowers with a darker red, emphasizing the edges of the petals. The details of the birds' faces are painted in burnt umber rather than black, to produce a softer effect – all that is needed for each bird is a small squiggle for the eye and a suggestion of a tucked-in beak. Add a white centre to each flower with just a touch of white paint on each petal.

STEP 5

Mix a light grey wash to add shading to the doves. Paint a little of this under their chests, imagining the light to come from the top left-hand corner. Pick out highlights in white, highlighting their foreheads, the upper part of the chest of the dove on the right-hand side which would be facing the light, the back of the head of the left-hand one, and their tails, again taking the brush strokes from the tip of the tail upwards, in this case just halfway up to the body.

STEP 6

Finish by adding a touch of shading to the leaves, mixing up a slightly darker shade of green and, again imagining the light to be coming from the left, thereby putting in shadows at the right-hand side of the leaves and below.

STEP 7

When all the paint has dried, apply an antique finish, as for the Antiqued Paeony Cupboard, but using burnt umber as a colouring with a touch of white. Wipe the mixture carefully around the doves, leaving them uncovered to keep them as white as possible and preserve the highlights.

On the following pages you will find listed all the materials used for the individual projects throughout the book. To enable you to reproduce our designs exactly, we have given exact details of brush sizes and paint colours. However, these are really only intended as suggestions and hopefully you will enjoy creating your own colour schemes, perhaps to coordinate with an existing decorative scheme in your own home.

The patterns you will find are also only intended as general guidelines for you to adapt or alter according to your requirements or creative needs. You will find information and advice on scaling patterns up and down on page 16. Many of the patterns will simply form the inspiration for your own ideas rather than be copied down to the last detail. If you do wish to reproduce one of our projects exactly, you will often find that the designs are so easy that they can be copied freehand. We hope that these practical details will provide a valuable insight into the projects on the preceding pages and that above all, they will give you the confidence to have fun with your own experiments.

DECORATIVE EGGS
Pages 38-41

The three egg patterns are each drawn freehand, as described.

MATERIALS
Red and pink egg
Base colour: pale pink silk vinyl or oil-based eggshell
Design colours: crimson acrylic tube; gloss varnish with burnt sienna acrylic
Brushes: watercolour sable or sable mixture, no. 0 or 1; also a pencil

Blue & green egg
Base colour: pale beige satin vinyl or oil-based eggshell
Design colours: acrylic tubes – turquoise, Hooker's green, Monestial blue
Brushes: watercolour sable or sable mixture, no. 1 or 2; also a black waterproof pen

Black & gold egg
Base colour: pale coffee satin vinyl or eggshell
Design colours: acrylic tubes – black, burnt umber, and Plaka gold
Brushes: watercolour sable or sable mixture brush, no. 0 or 1

FRAME WITH RIBBONS AND FRONDS
Pages 42-5

There is such a variety of frames to choose from that the basic pattern will almost inevitably require some adjustment, with the loops made deeper or more elongated to fill the size and shape of the frame. Use the mitred joins at the corners as guidelines when turning. The strawberry tablemat on page 90 is drawn in a very similar way and the pattern could easily be substituted for those shown here.

MATERIALS
Base colours: white acrylic undercoat, followed by coffee eggshell
Design colours: acrylic tubes – raw sienna, burnt umber, white, Plaka gold
Brushes: 4cm (1½in) household brush; watercolour sable or sable mixture, nos. 2, 4 and 6

NEW LAMPS FOR OLD –
SPONGED CERAMICS
Pages 46-9

No pattern is required for
the lamp base – the aim
should be to achieve a
random base colour, with
as many or as few rows of
spirals as suits the size and
shape of the lamp.

MATERIALS
Design colours: Pebeo à
l'eau – emerald, lavender
and white, and bronze
powder
Brush: imitation sable,
square-cut brush, 6mm
(¼in) wide and 1.2cm
(½in) long; also a small
natural sponge

HAND-PAINTED WALL FRIEZE
Pages 50-53

The square pattern guide is cut from thin card and acts as a guide within which you can draw the heart shape. One way to make sure that the template is drawn absolutely accurately is to draw it on graph paper, cut out a little outside the outline and glue this to card. You can then cut the template shape out, using a scalpel.

The pattern shows the basic design, as given in the project, plus a variation in which more hearts are fitted into the gaps of the first row to make a deeper frieze that would be suitable for a room with very high ceilings. A corner pattern, with four small hearts, is also given. This could be used either at the four corners of a panel, as shown in the picture, or at the corners of a room.

MATERIALS
Base colour: coral/peach
eggshell or silk vinyl
Design colours: cream silk
vinyl; acrylic tubes — white
and burnt umber
Brushes: watercolour sable
or sable mixture, nos 4
and 8

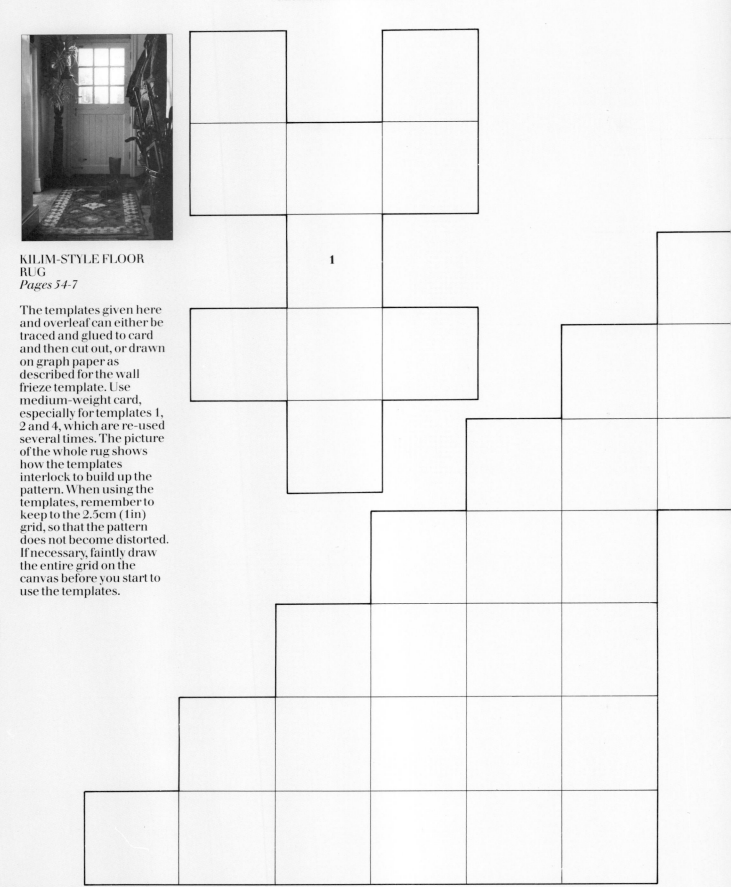

KILIM-STYLE FLOOR RUG
Pages 54-7

The templates given here and overleaf can either be traced and glued to card and then cut out, or drawn on graph paper as described for the wall frieze template. Use medium-weight card, especially for templates 1, 2 and 4, which are re-used several times. The picture of the whole rug shows how the templates interlock to build up the pattern. When using the templates, remember to keep to the 2.5cm (1in) grid, so that the pattern does not become distorted. If necessary, faintly draw the entire grid on the canvas before you start to use the templates.

MATERIALS
Base colour: acrylic gesso
Design colours: cream silk
vinyl; PVA or acrylic tubes –
Prussian blue, viridian,
crimson, orange, burnt
umber and burnt sienna
Brushes: 5cm (2in)
household brush; hog's
hair square or filbert-
tipped brush, no. 8 or 9;
sable square oil brush,
no. 6

2

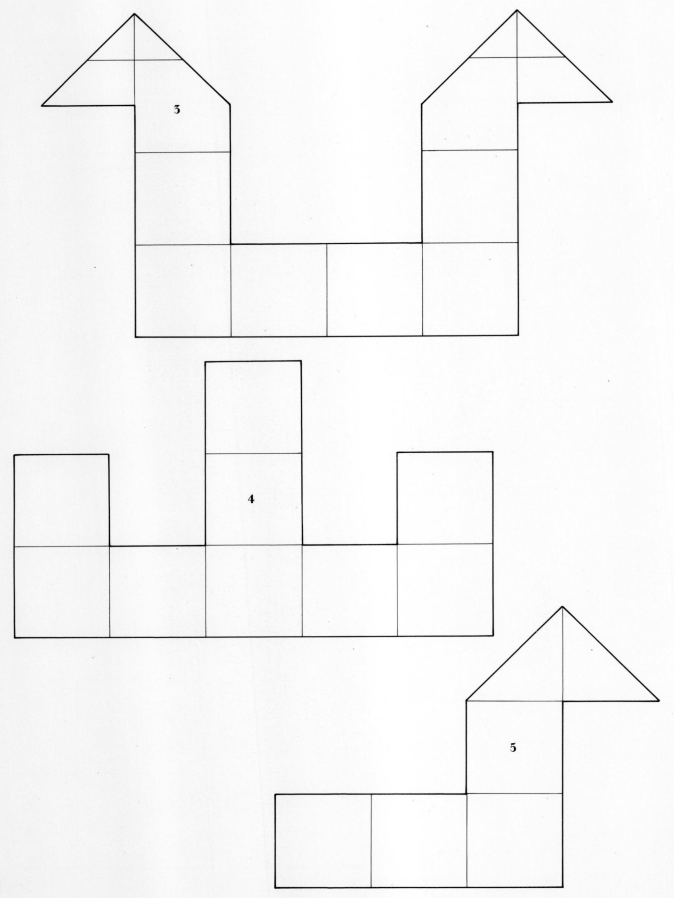

ROSES AND DAISIES –
BREAD BIN AND COOKIE
JAR
Pages 60-65

If you are painting this
pattern on a bread bin or
similar metal item, it is best
to draw the oval shape
then fill in the remainder
of the pattern freehand.

To draw the template
on a bin, the distance
between the handles of
your bread bin should be
measured to find the exact
centre point between
them and a vertical line
chalked down the bin
through this point. The
template is placed on the
bin, with vertical centre
points matching, and the
oval is drawn. The
horizontal centre points on
either side of the oval are
also marked on the bin. To
find the centre points of an
oval, enclose it in a
rectangle and mark off the
centres as normal.

This pattern can be
easily adjusted by adding
more flowers, changing
the shape of the centre
panel to a circle or hexagon, or simply applying a
different style of flower.

For the cookie jar, you
can draw the entire pattern
on a card template, scaling
it up or down to the size of
your jar.

MATERIALS

Bread bin
Base colour: dark blue
Hammerite
Design colours: acrylic
tubes – white, yellow
ochre, raw sienna, burnt
umber, Hooker's green,
Plaka gold
Brushes: 2.5cm (1in)
household brush;
watercolour sable or sable
mixture, nos 2, 4 and 6

Cookie jar
Design colours: Pebeo
Ceramic à Froid – yellow,
white, Victoria green,
turquoise, Sèvres
Brushes: watercolour sable
or sable mixture, nos 2, 4
and 6

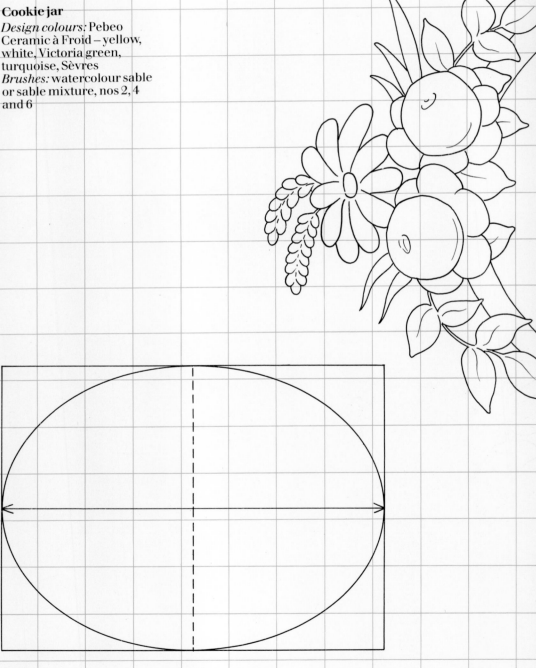

A B C D
E F G H I
J K L M
N O P Q
R S T U V
W X Y Z

abcdefghi
jklmnopq
rstuvwxyz

abcdefghijklm
nopqrstuvwxyz

1234567890

ANTIQUED PAEONY CUPBOARD
Pages 66-71

The shaped top of the frame that surrounds this picture is drawn as described in Step 1 of the main copy.

The pattern can be drawn freehand, but if you wish to copy it, the simplest way would be to draw a grid in chalk on your cupboard door and transfer the main outlines only, square for square. The details of the petals are filled in freehand, for a natural effect.

The pattern can easily be adjusted to a square door, as shown here, by leaving out the topmost flowers.

MATERIALS
Base colours: white gloss; dark green eggshell; greyish cream eggshell; apricot silk vinyl with PVA or acrylic tubes in red and burnt sienna
Design colours: acrylic tubes – white, Hooker's green, yellow ochre, cadmium red, Monestial blue, raw umber; antique glaze
Brushes: 5cm (2in) household brush; hog's hair square or filbert-tipped brush, no. 8; watercolour sable or sable mixture, nos 2, 4 and 6

OLD-ROSE CHEST OF DRAWERS
Pages 72-7

You may wish to create a design of your own, to match your own furnishings, but if you intend to use the design shown here, it should be drawn in two stages. The outline shapes should be drawn after the base coat (grey-green paint) has been applied. The flower pattern can be scaled up and transferred directly to grids drawn in chalk on the furniture only after the centre shapes have been filled in with the cream background.

The outlines that encompass the designs – diamonds on the top and end panels and a diamond-ended shape on the drawer fronts – may need to be altered to suit your furniture. The design inside can easily be adapted – by either repeating or removing some of the elements. To plot the shape on a drawer front, find the centre points at each side and join them, making a horizontal line across the drawer. Decide how far in from the top and bottom edges of the drawer you wish the horizontal outer lines of the design to run – ours were set in 2.5cm (1in) from the top and bottom respectively. Draw these lines right across the drawer. You now have

three horizontal lines across the drawer front: mark on the central line where you wish the point of the design outline to lie (ours were set in 4cm/1½in from the edge at each side), then measure in from each side along the top and bottom lines and mark where the sloping lines will meet the top and bottom lines (our angles were set in 9cm/3½in from each side). Draw the sloping lines to complete the shape.

The straightforward diamond shapes were made by drawing in the central horizontal and vertical lines, marking points in from the edges (here, 5cm/2in in from the sides and 7.5cm/3in in from the top and bottom) and then joining the points with a chalk and ruler.

Only one drawer pattern is given here, but if you look at the actual chest, you will notice that the pattern has been altered so that each drawer is slightly different. This can easily be done by changing the arrangement of the roses and adding or subtracting leaves and buds to fit the width and depth of each drawer.

MATERIALS
Base colours: white oil-based or acrylic undercoat; pale greyish green silk vinyl; cream silk vinyl
Design colours: acrylic tubes – turquoise, Hooker's green, Payne's grey, cadmium red light, cadmium yellow, white, burnt umber, lemon yellow
Brushes: 5cm (2in) household brush; hog's hair square or filbert-tipped, no. 8 or 10; coachliner, no. 4 and 6 (or large and medium); watercolour sable or sable mixture, nos 2, 4 and 9

FANTASY FLOWER
TABLECLOTH
Pages 78-81

The pattern can be copied directly, though you may find it easier to draw it freehand. Whichever you choose to do, start by folding the circular cloth into quarters and ironing it.

To copy the pattern exactly, measure the radius of your cloth and divide it by the number of divisions on the radius of the grid pattern shown here, to find the size of the squares for your full-size grid. On a large sheet of paper, draw up a grid to this size and scale up the pattern onto it.

Place the pattern over the fabric and sandwich a sheet of dressmakers' carbon paper, carbon side down, between the two. Trace over the pattern, then repeat the process for the three remaining quarters.

If you wish to draw the pattern freehand, use chalk and draw a long S shape, as shown. Next, draw lateral branches and leaves from the central S-shaped stem, then fill in the flower outlines.

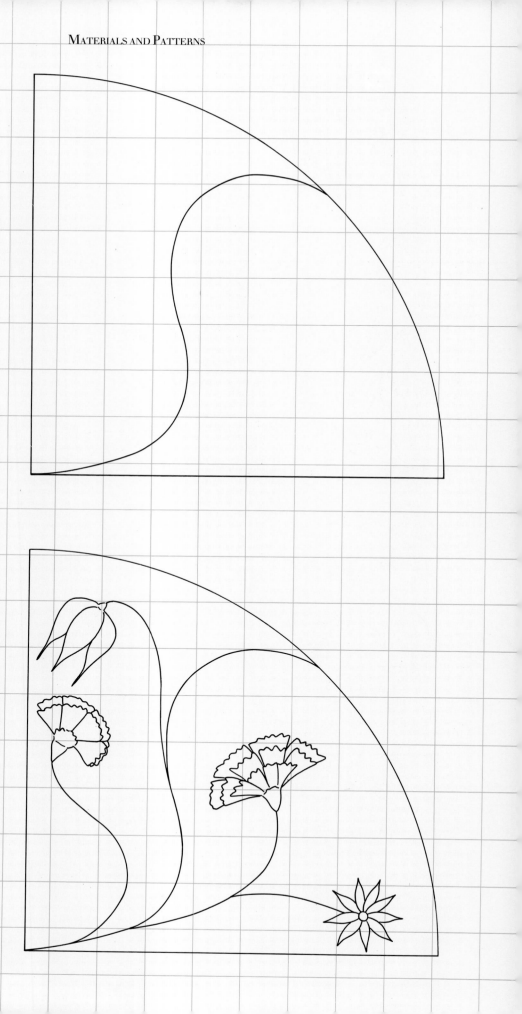

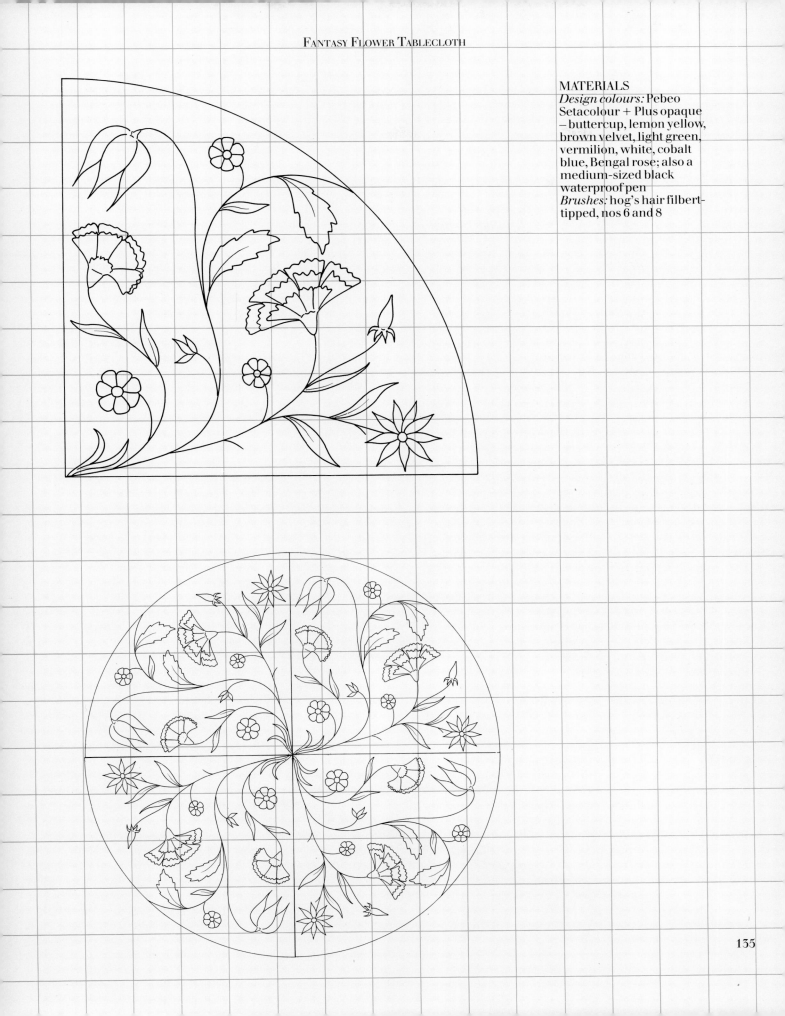

MATERIALS
Design colours: Pebeo
Setacolour + Plus opaque
– buttercup, lemon yellow,
brown velvet, light green,
vermilion, white, cobalt
blue, Bengal rose; also a
medium-sized black
waterproof pen
Brushes: hog's hair filbert-
tipped, nos 6 and 8

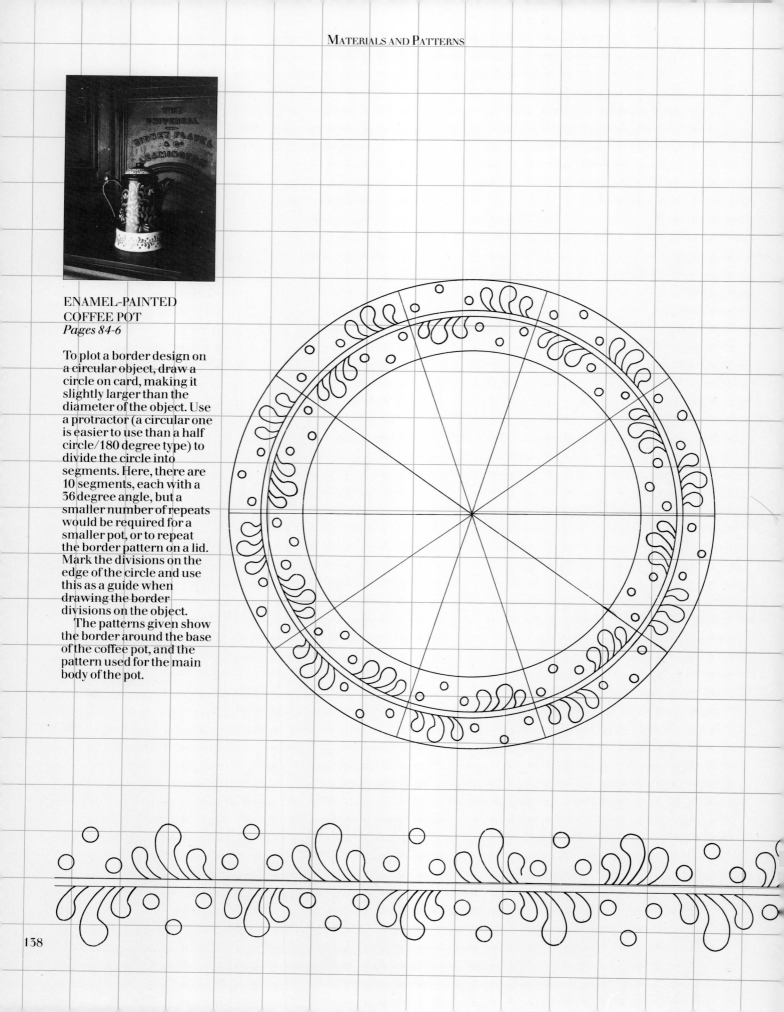

ENAMEL-PAINTED COFFEE POT
Pages 84-6

To plot a border design on a circular object, draw a circle on card, making it slightly larger than the diameter of the object. Use a protractor (a circular one is easier to use than a half circle/180 degree type) to divide the circle into segments. Here, there are 10 segments, each with a 36 degree angle, but a smaller number of repeats would be required for a smaller pot, or to repeat the border pattern on a lid. Mark the divisions on the edge of the circle and use this as a guide when drawing the border divisions on the object.

The patterns given show the border around the base of the coffee pot, and the pattern used for the main body of the pot.

MATERIALS
Base colours: matt black
spray car paint; white
Japlac enamel
Design colours: Humbrol
gloss model paints
(enamel) – bright green,
pale green, bright red and
white
Brushes: hog's hair square
or filbert-tipped, nos 4
and 6; watercolour sable
or sable mixture, nos 2, 4
and 6

EXOTIC FRUITS KITCHEN PANEL
Pages 87-9

Additional fruits, as shown, can easily be added to those in the existing design or they could be used on their own to echo the theme on smaller objects. Use chalk to draw the pattern on the cupboard door. First find the centre point of the cupboard by finding the centre points of the sides and the top and bottom and drawing a centre line across and another down the door. You can crosscheck that this is the true centre by drawing in the diagonals. Matching up the centre point of the door to the centre of the grid, draw a grid of 10cm (4in) squares on the door and transfer the outlines of the fruit and leaves.

If you wish to work freehand, using the pattern as a general guide only, you may find that it helps if you chalk in an oval on the door and work within this as a general outline. A meat dish or similar plate may be a suitable size and shape to use when drawing the outline. It will also help if you draw in the centre lines across the door. The advantage of working a design like this freehand is that you can adapt it to the shape of the door and you will also find it easier to achieve the flowing, natural effect.

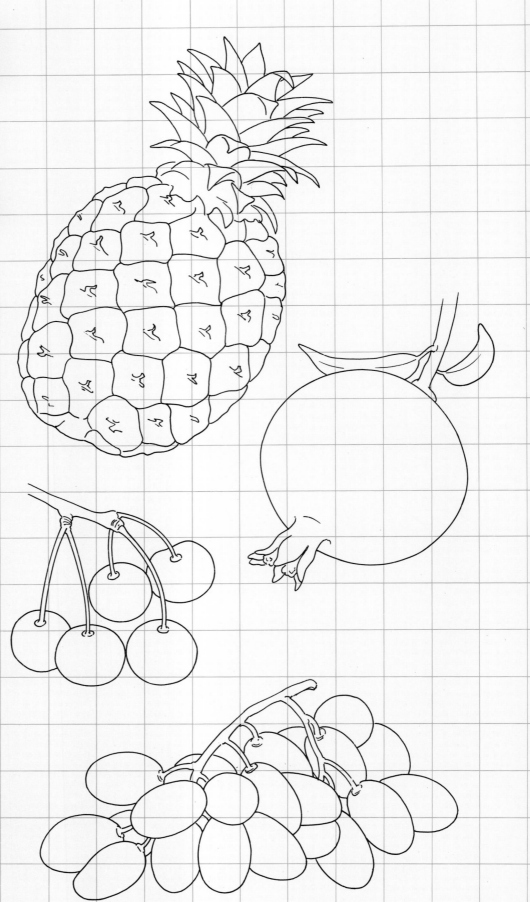

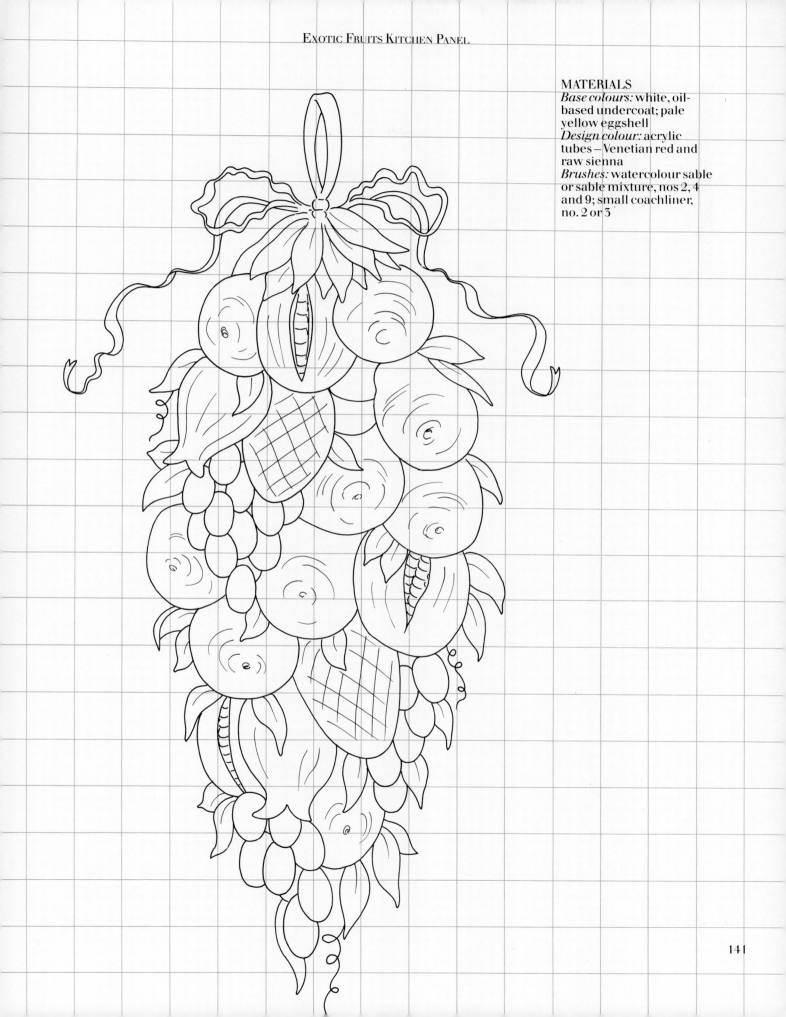

MATERIALS
Base colours: white, oil-based undercoat; pale yellow eggshell
Design colour: acrylic tubes – Venetian red and raw sienna
Brushes: watercolour sable or sable mixture, nos 2, 4 and 9; small coachliner, no. 2 or 3

STRAWBERRY CIRCLE
Pages 90-93

For the most part this design is more easily painted freehand than by painstakingly following a pattern, but it is important to make sure that the divisions of the design are planned and marked out carefully, so that the finished design will look attractive and well balanced. First use compasses to draw a circle, with a radius 3mm (⅛in) greater than the size of a mat, using a pencil and drawing it on card. Use a protractor to mark this into ten sections, each with a 36 degree angle, as described for the coffee pot border on page 138.

MATERIALS
Base colours: white oil-based or acrylic undercoat; yellow eggshell or silk vinyl
Design colours: acrylic tubes – Hooker's green, cadmium red, white, cadmium yellow
Brushes: 2.5cm (1in) household brush; watercolour sable or sable mixture, nos 2 and 4; coachliner, no. 2 or small

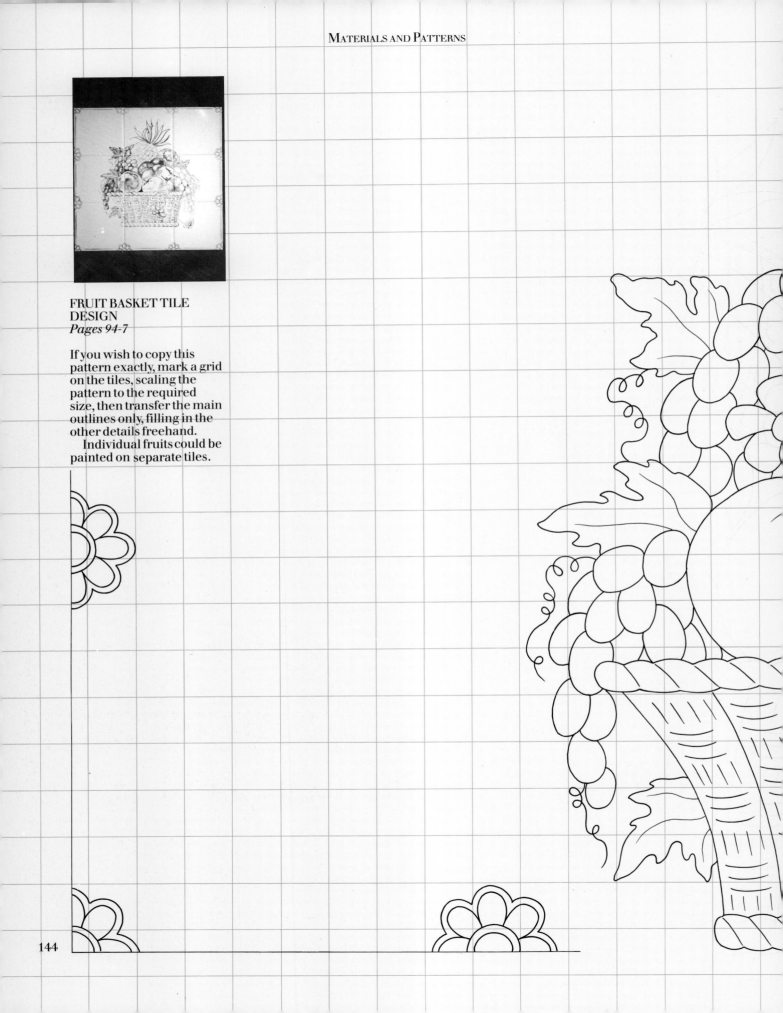

FRUIT BASKET TILE DESIGN
Pages 94-7

If you wish to copy this pattern exactly, mark a grid on the tiles, scaling the pattern to the required size, then transfer the main outlines only, filling in the other details freehand.

Individual fruits could be painted on separate tiles.

MATERIALS
Design colours: Pebeo
ceramic à l'eau – lavender,
Sèvres and black
Brushes: watercolour sable
or sable mixture, nos 2, 4
and 9

JUGGLING CLOWN APRON
page 100-102

Fold the apron in two from top to bottom and iron a crease. Decide exactly where you would like the clown's nose to go, allowing room at the top for the rest of his face and his juggling balls, then iron a crease from side to side and mark the centre point with a chalk cross. With the nose positioned on the cross, the clown can be drawn freehand using a soft pencil – the bright paint will later hide these outlines. Drawing is easier than it looks, but if you prefer to transfer the pattern, follow the instructions on page 16. We started with a circle for the nose and built up the rest symmetrically to the face, then drew in the collar, body and arms and legs. Next we did the stripes on his clothes, his hat, flower, feet and the balls. Drawing the clown in this order means that you can adjust the lengths of the legs or hands if he doesn't fit the space.

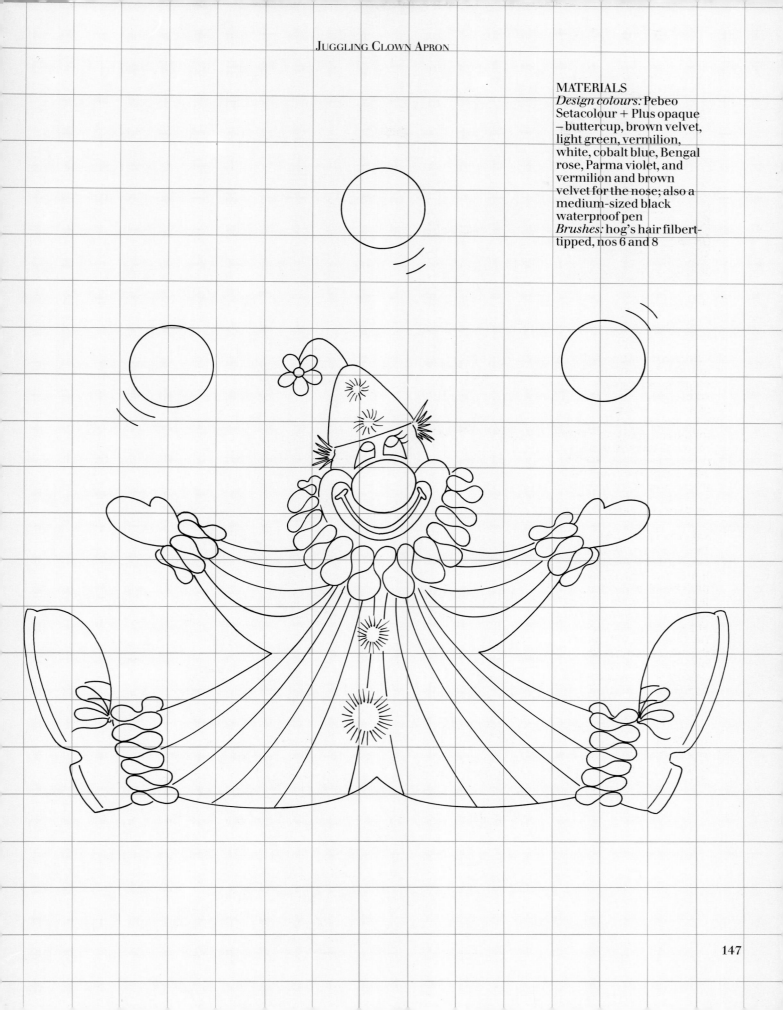

MATERIALS
Design colours: Pebeo
Setacolour + Plus opaque
– buttercup, brown velvet,
light green, vermilion,
white, cobalt blue, Bengal
rose, Parma violet, and
vermilion and brown
velvet for the nose; also a
medium-sized black
waterproof pen
Brushes: hog's hair filbert-
tipped, nos 6 and 8

TEDDY BEAR ROLLER BLIND
Pages 103-5

The teddy bears are all exactly the same, the only differences being that some are reversed, and there are two different sizes. If you have access to a photocopying machine that can make enlargements and reductions, you could use it to save yourself the trouble of drawing up the same motif to two sizes.

MATERIALS
Design colours: Pebeo Setacolor + Plus opaque – buttercup, brown velvet, light green, vermilion, white, cobalt blue, Bengal rose; also a medium-sized black waterproof pen
Brushes: hog's hair filbert-tipped, nos 6, 8 and 10

HEARTS, FLOWERS AND LOVERS
Pages 106-9

The painting of the lady is alternated with the kneeling man. Both can easily be drawn freehand, as described in the steps, but if you wish to copy the figures exactly, draw a chalk grid on each side of the waste paper basket and then copy the pattern square for square, rubbing away the chalked grid lines before you start to paint.

The corner pattern given here could easily be adapted to fit a basket of a slightly different shape.

MATERIALS
Base colours: white acrylic or oil-based undercoat; turquoise-blue eggshell; red eggshell gloss (for inside)
Design colours: acrylic tubes – white, turquoise, yellow ochre, cadmium red light, Hooker's green, Payne's grey
Brushes: 4cm (1½in) household brush; large coachliner, no. 5 or 6; watercolour sable or sable mixture, nos 2, 4 and 8

Hearts, Flowers and Lovers

TURTLE DOVE CHAIR
Pages 110-113

This is a mirror image pattern, with the left and right halves of the picture reflecting each other. One way to transfer the pattern to a chair seat would be to scale up the outline for one half only of the heart onto tracing paper and cut around this outline and down the central dividing line. Repeat to make an outline pattern for one dove, then draw around these templates on the chair seat, turning them over to draw the second half of the pattern.

MATERIALS
Base colours: white oil-based or acrylic undercoat; greyish cream eggshell; antique glaze
Design colours: acrylic tubes – white, Hooker's green, cadmium red light, burnt umber, Payne's grey
Brushes: 2.5-4cm (1-1½in) household brush; watercolour sable or sable mixture, nos 9, 4 and 2

GLOSSARY

A

Acanthus Herbaceous plant with prickly leaves, popularly stylized as a decorative motif.
Acrylic A polymer based on synthetic resin. Acrylic paint is water based, the pigment dispersed in acrylic emulsion. It is non-toxic, tough and quick to dry.
Antiquing A method of rubbing down and/or applying dark paints or varnishes to make an object look much older than it really is.
Apex The top or tip; the peak of a triangle or a cone shape.

B

Bargeware Gaily painted everyday utensils used on the Victorian canal boats.
Baroque Exuberant, sometime grotesque or elaborate style, popular in the 17th and 18th centuries.
Batik A means of producing multi-coloured designs on textiles using wax on the parts that are not to be dyed any particular shade.

C

Caustic Soda Sodium hydroxide – chemical used to strip paint off timber objects or to age them prematurely.
Circumference The outside area measurement described by a circle or oval.
Coachliner Long-bristled paint brush designed for painting a straight line with a steady hand.
Compasses An instrument for drawing correct circles.
Coordinated A term used to describe patterns, colours, shapes or styles that look good together.

D

Dado The area of wall roughly between waist and floor level.
Delft A style of hand-painted glazed earthenware made at Delft in Holland, particularly in the 17th and 18th centuries.
Diameter A measurement passing through the centre from one side of an object to another.
Distemper A powdery paint applied to internal walls.

Dragging A broken paint effect using thinned paint and a large brush.

E

Eggshell Oil based paint with a soft sheeny finish.
Enamel Silicate based paint suitable for painting metal.

F

Ferrule The metal hair or bristle holder of a brush.
Filbert A cone-shaped brush.
Firing Objects subjected to heat to permanently fix a paint or glaze.
Fitch A long bristled brush (originally of polecat) used for painting straight lines.
Frieze A horizontal or sometimes vertical decorative band applied to a wall between architrave and cornice; below the ceiling or at dado level.

G

Gloss Paint with shiny finish.

H

Hammered Finish Metal paint with dimpled effect finish.
Herringbone Zigzag pattern.
Hexagon A shape with six sides and angles.

J

Japan A lacquer with a hard varnish finish.

K

Key (a surface) To roughen a surface to help the next coat of paint or varnish to adhere.

L

Lozenge A rhomboid diamond shape.

154

M

Matt A dull, lustre-less finish.
MDF Medium Density Fibreboard.
Monochromatic A scheme based on shades of a single colour.

O

Opaque Not transparent, milky.

P

Paint Kettle A tin into which paint may be transferred for mixing or for easier application with the brush.
Pantograph A manual instrument for copying a plan or design to any scale.
Pastel Any pale shade.
Plumb Bob A ball of lead or other weight attached to string to determine an accurate vertical line.
Plywood Thin but strong board made by gluing layers of timber together with the grains crosswise.
Polyurethane Paints based on synthetic resin or strong synthetic varnish.
Primary A basic colour – red, yellow or blue – in its pure form.
Primer Paint or other substance used to seal a surface before painting.
Protractor An instrument for measuring angles.
PVA Paint based on acrylic or synthetic resin.

R

Rag Rolling A broken paint effect created with a screwed-up rag.
Romany Gipsy style.
Rosemaling A flower painting technique characteristic of Norwegian folk art.

S

Scumble A medium used to thin paint to produce a softer, more opaque effect or apply a broken paint technique.
Shellac A form of varnish.
Silhouette A profile of an object showing outline only.

Silk Finish A satin or soft sheen effect.
Spirit Level An instrument used to test the accuracy of vertical or horizontal lines.
Sponging A broken paint effect applied with a natural sponge.
Sugar Soap An abrasive substance for cleaning off dirt and grease or removing paint.

T

Tear Stroke A one-move paint technique producing a tapered teardrop shape.
Template A pattern or guide.
Tole An early American decorative tradition applied to furniture and everyday objects.
Translucent Transmitting light but not quite transparent.
Trompe l'oeil A painting designed to deceive the eye with its realism.
Turpentine A pungent oil used for mixing paints and varnishes.

V

Van Dyking Decorative painting technique used by canal boat dwellers to decorate their boats and belongings.

W

Wash A thinned application of paint.
White Spirit Turpentine substitute.
Wirewool A type of scourer.

Z

Zinc Chromate A metal primer used to stabilize rust-prone surfaces ready for painting.

USEFUL ADDRESSES

ARTISTS' MATERIALS

Cowling & Wilcox, 26 Broadwick Street, London W1
Tel: 01 734 9556

Daler-Rowney Ltd, PO Box 10, Southern Industrial
Estate, Bracknell, Berks RG12 4ST
Tel: 0344 424621

Green & Stone, 259 Kings Road, London SW3
Tel: 01 352 0837

Green & Stone of Cirencester, 19 West Market Place,
Cirencester, Glos GL7 2AE
Tel: 0285 69085

The London Graphic Centre (Pebeo), Long Acre,
Covent Garden, London WC2
Tel: 01 240 0235

Reeves Art Shop, 178 Kensington High Street,
London W8
Tel: 01 937 5370

A West & Partners Ltd (Pebeo), 684 Mitcham Road,
Croydon, Surrey CR9 3AB
Tel: 01 684 6171

SCUMBLE GLAZE

Craig & Rose plc, Princes Road, Dartford,
Kent DA2 6EE
Tel: 0322 21372

J T Keep & Sons, 15 Theobalds Road, London WC1
Tel: 01 242 0313

MANUFACTURERS

The manufacturers listed below offer information and
advice about their products.

Crown Paints, PO Box 37, Crown House, Hollins Road,
Darwin, Lancs BB3 0BG
Tel: 0254 74951

Dulux, Imperial Chemical Industries plc,
Slough SL2 5DS
Tel: 0753 31151

Dylon International Ltd (Fabric), Worsley Bridge
Road, Lower Sydenham, London SE26 5HD
Tel: 01 836 6677

Sterling Roncraft, 15 Churchfield Court, Churchfield,
Barnsley, S. Yorks S70 2LJ
Tel: 0226 207676

INDEX

ACKNOWLEDGMENTS

My thanks to David Palliser who helped with the text and
tolerated my deadlines; to Angela Gair who helped
initially to tie the ends together, to Denis Kennedy who
stayed reasonably calm and to Diana Mansour who
finally got the whole thing organized and making sense.
A very special thanks to Belinda Ballantine for doing such
a marvellous job against the clock on the majority of
projects and for her inestimable patience and good
temper. Thanks also to Sarah Baxter for her artistic
talents and help with the projects. We are also grateful to
all those companies and individuals listed below, who
contributed advice, information, materials or
photographic material.

The mirror frame used for the project 'Frame with
Ribbons and Fronds' can be made to order by The Rowley
Gallery, 115 Kensington Church Street, London W8 7LN.

The fabric that inspired the design of the 'Old-Rose Chest
of Drawers' was 'Ludlow' by Ramm Son & Crocker,
Treadway Hill, Loudwater, High Wycombe,
Bucks HP10 9PE.

PICTURE CREDITS